Fredrick H. Shurly

Why Believe in God?

WHY BELIEVE IN GOD?

PETER ANTHONY BERTOCCI

A Keen-Age Reflection Book

ASSOCIATION PRESS

NEW YORK

WHY BELIEVE IN GOD?

———————

Copyright © 1963 by
National Board of Young Men's Christian Associations

———————

Association Press, 291 Broadway, New York 7, N. Y.

Price, 50 cents

Publisher's title stock number: 556
Library of Congress catalog card number: 63-10382

Printed in the United States of America

Preface

Why should I believe in God? This question is not a rebellious "declaration of independence" by immature minds. It is a question a person asks when he finds himself believing or disbelieving in God, without knowing exactly why. It is a question that thinking persons of every age ask when they decide to take stock of beliefs that have made "all the difference" either in their own lives or in the lives of others whom they respect. It is a question asked by all who want to understand the meaning of their own lives in the world as they know it.

How might one go about answering this question? There is more than one way that thoughtful men have approached the problem of belief in God. Let me indicate briefly the approach to be taken in this book.

The argument here does not depend on what one's past or present religious commitment is. While reference is made to Jewish and Christian belief in God as found in the Old and New Testaments, I do not argue *from* that experience and belief. If anything, I argue *to* basic convictions in the Judeo-Christian view of God. The argument, in other words, proceeds from considerations open to all reflective persons.

Special attention is paid to obstacles to belief, including some advanced in the name of science. Indeed, I try to show that some of the basic reasoning involved in the scientific pursuit of truth is in fact part of the reasoning for believing that God is a loving Creator.

He who wants a decisive, all-or-nothing proof will be disappointed. The considerations we shall have before us are intended to help one find his way to reasonable, but not foolproof, belief. What is "reasonable belief"? To answer that, and similar questions, is the purpose of this book.

PETER A. BERTOCCI

Arlington, Massachusetts

Contents

Why Believe in God?

1

Which God?

Is Religious Belief "a Private Matter"?

It does not matter for the discussion in this book what your religious background is. Still, nobody can think about religion without keeping in mind the variety of belief about God. If you are a Protestant, you may belong to one of the six largest Protestant Christian denominations in this country: Baptist (21,374,126), Methodist (12,585,394), Presbyterian (4,277,947), Episcopal (3,444,265), Congregationalist (2,022,090), or to one of the 250 (roughly) remaining Protestant sects in America. You may be one of the 42,104,899 Roman Catholics, or one of the 2,718,110 Eastern Orthodox Christians.*

Whatever your religious upbringing, there are other people equally sincere who will believe in God,

---

* In rough numbers, there are about 214,000,000 Christians in the world, which is half as many as Moslems. Confucians and Hindus each number a third more than Christians, and Buddhists approximate two-thirds the number of Christians. These five great world religious groups comprise only half of the three billion people who have some recorded affiliation.

but not in your God. Nevertheless, the fact that roughly three billion people prefer some religious faith is not one to be brushed aside lightly. And all of us, sooner or later, find ourselves asking: Why believe in God anyway?

The answer, we shall see, is not a simple one. And often it seems easier to be "broad-minded" and set the whole question aside with some such remark as: "Whether one believes in God, what he thinks about God, is a private matter. Let other people believe what they want, and let me believe as I wish—as long as we are each free to believe or not to believe in his own way!"

Let us agree that there must be freedom to believe or not to believe, that every person must be free to make up his own mind. But can we dismiss the whole matter of religious faith by saying: Let each live his life in his own way? Don't we actually discover that another's religious belief or disbelief has a way of being far from his private business?

In America, for example, every coin bears the stamp "In God We Trust." When an American takes the "pledge of allegiance," he does not merely say: "I pledge allegiance to the flag of the United States of America and to the Republic for which it stands." He goes on to say, "one nation under God, indivisible, with liberty and justice for all." Can a thoughtful American leave it for other Americans to decide what form of "republic" we are to live in? Can he leave it to other Americans to decide for him what it means

to live "under God"? Indeed, what God should we
live under? Or, should we consent to live under any
God at all?

There are thinking people in America who believe
that justice and liberty do not require belief in God
—in fact, that there will be more justice and liberty
without belief in God. The governments of Russia
and of Communist China are based on the policy that
belief in God is like a drug that makes people in-
capable of demanding justice and liberty. Millions in
the newly rising nations are pondering the question:
Is belief in God justified? Does belief in God really
make a difference to the ideals of people?

No responsible member of any society, let alone
of the United States of America, can allow himself to
stand on the sidelines on this issue. The recent decision of the United States Supreme Court regarding
the requirement of prayer in public schools brings
every American back to careful consideration of the
kind of relation that should exist between Church
and State.

Vigorous people hate to be parasites—they do not
want to let others do all the thinking, or to live on
the beliefs of others. For many years I have taught
pre-college and college young people, and I have discovered one thing about most of those who do not
seem to take the question of God seriously. Seldom
has the question of God been presented to them as
one which they might *think* about in the same way
as they think about other problems. The fear of dis-

appointing parents and friends by "losing their faith," the emphasis placed upon the importance of "believing something"—as though not to believe is to betray—has discouraged many, young and old, from pursuing the questions that naturally come up about belief in God.

In this book we shall be as much concerned with the problem of how to think about religious faiths as with any specific conclusion about God. Though restricted space and the complexity of the subject will limit us to hardly more than a point of view, belief in God will not be taken for granted. We shall inquire what it means to believe in God, and whether belief does make a difference to the pursuit of truth or justice or liberty.

Which God Don't You Believe In?

When a person says "I believe in God," the question that immediately comes to my mind is: I wonder what kind of God he believes in? For the kind of God he believes in can make all the difference in the world to others as well as to himself. For example, a student writes that he believes God so planned it that women should be subservient to men (and he quotes Scripture to that effect). Another "believer" is flunking out of school because he will not buckle down to work that he actually can do. "God," he says, "has a purpose in making the faculty fail me. I know I'll get somewhere, for God will not let me down." There are millions the world over whose

"God" seems to support beliefs and actions that would be hard to justify by fact and reason.

But disbelievers in God can also be irresponsible about disbelieving what they want to disbelieve, with little help of reasoning. "If there is a God," said a sixteen-year-old skeptic, "why did he let our President Roosevelt die of a brain hemorrhage and let Stalin live?" What kind of a God would this young man approve? One who hurts our enemies and helps our friends?

And what God does the seventeen-year-old girl have in mind when she complains, "I prayed and prayed and prayed that God would save my brother in the Army, but he died after three weeks at the front. What's the use of praying? Anyway, if there is a God, why doesn't he make it impossible for us not to believe in him, and why doesn't he let bad things happen to the people who do not believe in him?"

Clearly both belief in God and disbelief in God may follow a person's own prescription. We believe or do not believe in a God who, we think, should act in accordance with our wishes.

But before going further, let's stop to ask ourselves: Why shouldn't we expect people to think wishfully about God? We all want our own wishes and our own beliefs supported by some authority outside ourselves. "Anyone with common sense knows . . ."; "Everybody says so!" When strong wishes are at stake, we are all good at manufacturing, out of shreds of cloth if not whole cloth, support for what we want to believe. And what greater authority can we appeal to than to God, even when we have made him in our own image!

So we can't help smiling when we hear the story of the young theological student who, despite the fact he had failed most tests at the seminary insisted: "But I know I can make a good preacher. For I saw clearly in the skies the letters GPC, telling me to "Go Preach Christ." A kindly old professor suggested, as tactfully as possible, that perhaps those letters were commanding "Go Plant Corn." Alas, it is only human to interpret God's "message" in the spirit of the young man who, rejected by the girl he loves, says, "She really loves me, she must love me, she will love me!"

Nevertheless, there is a lesson behind this so-called wishful thinking. To each believer a certain kind of God is important. "God," a specific God, seems to come into his life to fill needs which at that time he cannot bear to have disappointed. When it comes to what we value most—our loved ones, our life vocation, our crops, justice for all, the winning of a war— we cannot believe that "the powers that be" are against us. We connect God with what favors the best as we would have it and is against the worst as we see it. Thus our sense of the best shapes our concept of "our God." If we could collect all the very powerful wishes we have had at different times in our lives, wouldn't we probably have a good index to all of the different "Gods" we have expected to support us?

What is true of individuals in this case seems true of people generally and of nations. What a story the Old Testament tells us on this point! Discover the deep-seated wishes of a group, or the kinds of values people have come to believe are vital to their living. These wishes and values will account for their image of God. These yearnings, they will say, are pointers to God. God is "He who" satisfies these wants and aspirations. But they will also say, and with reason: "Nor would we have had these yearnings and aspirations if God had not made us what we are." A deep need assumes a God, not only to satisfy it but to account for it.

The Belief That Matters Most

It is easy to see, then, why many people accuse believers of creating God—and in their own image. Granted! Our image of God must be our image. But can't some of our images be better than others, or must all the images that men make be false? For example, are all the images that a child builds of his mother as he grows up equally false? Does "Mother" in fact support some of his beliefs better than others? This is the question.

In other words, just because each of us in his own lifetime has had more than one "God," and just because all over the world we can count many differing images and ideas of God, we cannot conclude that all ideas of God are equally false. Nor does it follow that the wish to find support for our values is a bad one. What question is more important to ask than: Are our values not only ours but rooted in the nature of things? If "God" is an answer to any of our questions, he is certainly connected with the answer to this one concerning values.

It seems clear: to think about God is to seek an answer to two questions: First, what must matter most to us? Second, how do we know that what matters most to us matters most to the structure of things? For whatever God is, if he exists, he exists as the source of the things that matter most to us.

But how can we know what matters most? To ask this question is to realize that whatever else matters, truth matters. We don't want simply to believe or disbelieve. We want truly to believe, and to believe the truth.

And so we must make an irksome detour when we are anxious to head straight for God. In our next chapter we must ask: How do we test the truth of any belief or disbelief in what matters most?

2

How Do We Justify a Belief?

Sense and Sensitivity

"Steve, have you been saying your prayers at night?" The seven-year-old, lying on his back in bed, looked up at his father with boyish embarrassment. For it was their custom to pray together at bedtime, but his father had been away frequently of late. The answer came rather petulantly: "Oh no! Daddy." His father, sensing that something was wrong, asked: "What's the matter, Steve?"

"Well, Daddy, I've been lying here night after night and saying, Hi, God! Hi, God! but I just didn't get any answer. So, I quit praying. If God is there, he isn't answering me! Why should I believe in him?"

What does one say to an argument like this? A ten-year-old, a teen-ager, a college student, a philosopher can ask the same question in different words. What is Steve's problem?

When Steve was left alone to find God, he soon found himself in difficulties. If there is a God, why can't I hear him, or see him, or touch him? Why can't I hear him as I do music or even the whistle of the wind? If he is supposed to be so close we can talk to him, why does he not talk to us?

A high school student in physics, chemistry, or biology might put the same question in this way: Why don't I observe God as I observe the things that take place in the test tube or under a microscope? If seeing is believing in science, why should it not be so in religion?

And he might add what a sixteen-year-old in junior high school once actually said: "After all, if you can't hear or see or touch God, aren't you likely to put God anywhere you want him? What is to keep you from imagining him in any way you wish? How are you going to know that when you say, 'God's there,' you are talking about God and not your own wishes!" The problem of our last chapter has come up again.

Well, Steve's question has become a bit more complicated, but it is in some ways the 64,000-dollar question. It figures heavily in philosophical debates about God's existence. Do we have any right to believe what we can never sense?

The conversation that ensued with Steve went something like this:

"Steve, do you believe that Daddy loves you?" (It is a risky question, but I trusted in our relationship.)

"Sure, Dad," said Steve, laughing.

"Well, Steve, do you *see*, or *hear* or *smell* or *touch* your own love for me?"

Being a seven-year old, Steve doesn't have all the words, and we had first to talk about what it was like to smell toast burning, to see it blacken, to touch its crispness, and so on. After a while I pressed the question.

"No, Dad, I can't see, hear, touch, smell, or taste my love for you."

"Well, Steve, do you know it exists in you?"

"Of course."

"Do you smell, see, touch, taste, hear my love for you, Steve?"

"No."

"Yet you believe it is there?"

"Yes."

"Well, Steve, I believe that God is love. It does not trouble me that I cannot smell, see, taste, hear, or touch him. It does not bother me if I do not hear, touch, smell, taste your love. I believe you love me not only because you tell me but because you act as I expect someone to act who loves me. How about it, Steve? You said that you called "Hi" to God and he did not answer you. Does this prove that God is not there?"

This took a bit of repeating, but it was not long before Steve said: "I get it!" And then, to my surprise, he added: "Taffy, my dog, loves me too. He can't talk the way we do, but he acts loving."

Perhaps Steve was convinced by too little. But our conversation was not intended to prove that God exists. It was intended to show that there are many things *we live by* that are not colored (or see-able), or accessible to us through our different senses. It was important for Steve at a very early age to understand what many people never seem to understand really, that human beings don't live only by the things they can eat, touch, see. We live not *by sense* alone, but *by sensitivity* to what we cannot sense.

Two Different Connected Worlds. of Sense and of Sensitivity

Our senses are very important, for they reveal what is immediately around us. We cannot escape from what they bring to us. We can readily understand why we come to think that what we sense "is there." But does it follow that only what we can sense is there, and believable?

Indeed, had Stephen been older and known arithmetic I might have tried to show him that even though he *said* and *heard* that $2 + 2 = 4$, he didn't believe this because he saw it with his eyes and heard it with his ears. He "saw" that two and two make four with his mind's eye, his "intelligence" or his "intellect." Our senses help us in figuring out our arithmetic problem, as when we count four apples that our eyes see, but the principle our intellect sees is that any two plus any other two makes four.

Later, also, Steve was to understand that we do not live only by the laws of things we sense—such as the law of gravitation and other laws in the physical and biological world—or only by the principles of arithmetic, for that matter.

I refer to situations not uncommon in family life.

Who has not heard the youngest child complain, "Mother, you gave him a bigger piece of pie than mine. Why should I not get as big a piece?" And when he adds the almost inevitable, "That's not fair," is he appealing to arithmetic or to smell, or sight, or touch alone? Or does he speak as if he were quite sure of something else which he did not contact through the senses or arithmetic, something we call "justice"?

We need not stop here to determine how we know that a given act is not fair, or just, or courageous. For our point is simply this. Anybody who says, "We live only in the world we sense," is telling only part of the truth. For we also live by rules of logic, which we cannot sense, and by principles of morality—of justice, honesty, kindness, which we cannot sense. Indeed, we live in our world of sense by using our principles of logic and morality!

We cannot, to be sure, check our conclusions in the field of logic and of morality as effectively as those we draw from the world we sense. In the world of test tubes, microscopes, telescopes, checking is easier to do and agreement is more readily arrived at than in the world where the senses don't reach. Nevertheless, can we escape the fact that people live also in the "world of sensitivity" in which the laws seem to be laws of reason, of love and justice and mercy, of hope and faith?

Consider, for example, what happens to us when we are very unjust, when we don't love, when we lose all hope. It may be harder to check principles of justice and love, but we certainly suffer serious consequences when we disregard them. If men had completely neglected "moral and spiritual laws," they would have destroyed each other already by the very scientific laws they could more readily check. Curiously enough, when nations do injure each other they do so by use of physical laws—and in the name of moral and spiritual ideals!

We live in two "worlds"—one of fact, the other of value. Prominent among "the facts" is the fact that our values influence what we do with our facts. Yet it is true that we cannot check on our values as readily, or in quite the same way, as we can check on our facts. It was this that really troubled our high school student.

What is "Matter of Fact"?

His question amounted to this: Once you get away from the things you can perceive with your senses, how do you know that you aren't just believing what you want to believe? I am going to suggest the answer in one preliminary sentence, try to explain what this means concretely, and then later show what it means for our thinking about God. *A belief about the existence of anything is true when it is more reasonable than any other belief.*

I can't demonstrate mathematically in $2 + 2 = 4$ fashion that I shall live until tonight. Nor can I prove logically—if A is greater than B, and B greater than C, then A *must be* greater than C—that because I am living as I write this sentence, I must live until to-night. I have more reason for believing that I'll live than for believing that I'll die. My doctor, who examined me last month, gave me a clean bill of health on the basis of his training, experience, and his observation; I might still be taken by a heart seizure or an accident, but the balance of evidence is in favor of my belief. The future will show whether my belief is true or not. But I hold it to be true *now* because there is too little evidence to the contrary.

Again, I believe, for example, that Columbus, Moses, and Abraham Lincoln lived between certain dates and did certain things. But I cannot be logically certain that these beliefs are true. History is certainly not "bunk," but it is far from easy to "get the facts" about the past. Persons who supposedly "recorded the facts" about Columbus, Moses, and Lincoln might have emphasized some events at the expense of others.

Yet such considerations do not keep me, however cautious they make me, from believing that some beliefs about these men are truer than others. I shall probably never know all there is to know about these men, but *I treat my beliefs as "facts" if they are based on evidence, if they are not inconsistent with other "known facts," and if they fit in with the other "established" evidence we do have.*

In other words, when we say that certain "matters of fact" are so, we are not talking about something we can prove beyond any question of a doubt (as that $2 + 2 = 4$). If "true" means "proved beyond a logical doubt," then, let us face it, there are very few, if any, *undeniable* "matter-of-fact" truths. When we say, "We live by truth," what we mean is that we live by what we believe is reasonable probability, the kind of probability just described.

Since I am going to suggest that belief in a certain kind of God is "true" in the same way, let us first consider other illustrations of this claim that truths of "matter of fact" are probable, but not logically necessary.

For instance, I believe that the earth is "round." This belief is much easier for me than it was for persons in Columbus' time. Then I might well have joined the scoffers who said "that man Columbus is a crackpot." It seemed so obvious that the earth was flat. But those people who boasted that "everyone who can use his eyes knows that the earth is flat" had not taken the trouble to collect even enough evidence from the senses. They had not really observed that on the ocean a vessel dips below the horizon. Had they been able to take more thoughtful account of the phases of the moon, of eclipses, and of other evidence we have, they would have come to question their belief more seriously.

We have here a perfect example of how a belief that seemed "so obvious" became less and less acceptable as sensible evidence accumulated. Today we prove it by sending airplanes around the earth, and we even take pictures of degrees of sphericity.

No, our reasoning about what our eyes see tells us

that we cannot "just believe our eyes." Thus, when we look at the moon, our eyes tell us that the moon is shining! But when we bring other observations to bear on this conclusion, we find it reasonable to change our minds. For if we hold that the moon has its own light, we can't explain what happens when we have eclipses of the sun, that is, when the moon is in our direct line of vision with the sun. As the moon begins to enter our line of vision to the sun, darkness (eclipse) begins to appear. If the moon had its own light, this would not happen. When the eclipse is total, the sun as we usually see it is blotted out, leaving its flaming coronas in view.

Our test (or criterion) of truth is, we now realize, not so much what we sense or don't sense, but whether our hypothesis fits the evidence better than any other hypothesis. Thus, our hypothesis—that the moon has no light of its own—is more probable than any other, or becomes a "matter of fact," because there is more evidence in its favor than for the contrary hypothesis. To put the same idea in different words, we can say that, thinking with this hypothesis, more of the evidence we have falls into place, sticks together—coheres—than would happen with any other hypothesis. Our reason for not believing that man came into existence in 6000 B.C. is that this belief does not fit most of the evidence. Our reason for not believing that the earth is created in six days or that man is not related in his biological evolution to the great apes, is that these hypotheses do not cohere with as much evidence as the ones we hold at present.

The only way we can keep our feelings from overcoming the evidence is by asking whether the relevant evidence fits in—is more coherent—with a given hypothesis than with any other—wish or no wish.

But I hear someone exclaim: Aren't you making too big a leap when you say that there is no difference *in kind* between truth about the physical world, the biological world, and truth in religion. This is an important question and needs more discussion than it can get here. But I suggest that what might be called "coherence of hypothesis and experience" is the test everywhere. However, as we shall see, it is one thing to say that there is one test for every field and another to say that in every area of life we can be equally "sure" of our "facts." For example, it is harder to check evidence about the past than about the present. Furthermore, at any stage of investigation in any field some evidence may be more dependable than other evidence. But my point is that in every field of life we trust, and rightly trust, hypotheses that help us to correlate our evidence and lead us to the discovery of other evidence.

The truths we live by are never more than reasonably probable. We may think we live by certainties, but we find we guide our lives by different degrees of probability. *We don't live probably, but we guide our living by probability!* We reason on the basis of evidence we have, and hope for the best. But we never live by certainty. At best we *feel certain* about a given hypothesis.

Can it be that in religion we can escape living by probability (truth)? We had better reserve final judgment on this until we look at more evidence. This much we can say now. While religious people live by the certainty they feel, the whole problem is to justify that "feeling of certainty." For equally "certain" religious people believe different things. In order to check the possibility that our certainty is not wishful thinking, we can ask: Is our belief (or unbelief) more coherent with available evidence than any other belief? Is the weight of evidence in its favor or not? If it is, we are justified in living by our reasonable faith.

To summarize: when we try to justify a belief we proceed to show the evidence that we have for it. We realize that we may never have all the evidence we might like, that some legitimate doubt is always possible. Yet we consider a belief "true," that is, truer than other beliefs, until some other evidence comes to light that will justify changing our belief. The way in which we keep ourselves from wishful (or antiwishful) thinking is to gather the relevant evidence for competing hypotheses and live by the one that is most coherent with the evidence at hand.

3

How Do We Justify
Faith-for-Living?

"Matter of Faith"

If we could watch the responsible scientist closely as he observes and experiments, we would see that he has to protect himself from allowing his hunches and preferences to bias his observations and conclusions. This "protection" is much harder in some kinds of scientific observations than others. What goes on in the test tube goes on independently of him; he cannot change what is happening. What goes on in the retort does not go on in him, although it may disappoint him. It is much easier for him then to be "objective," for once the experiment is on he can only "wait and see." Scientific method, in such situations or in more complicated ones, is intended to keep him out of "what's happening" as far as possible.

But in most of the hard choices human beings have to make in living, they themselves are part of the experiment. It is very important to know the "truth" in these situations, but it is very difficult, because the observer is in the very situation about which he seeks the truth. Let us consider three examples.

Suppose someone accuses my fifteen-year-old son of cheating at school. My first reaction is to refuse to believe it. I find myself wanting "absolute proof." The teacher shows me the papers in question, my son's and another boy's who sat next to him in the examination. "That explains it," I almost involuntarily say. "The other boy copied from my boy."

But the teacher shows me that my son's record in that class to date, in contrast to the other boy's, has been rather poor. Indeed, what made the teacher suspect cheating in the first place was the remarkable improvement in this paper. I discover that the papers are in fact quite similar. To the practiced eye some of the wording in my son's paper strikes a somewhat false note, even though it is not wrong.

Both boys swear they did not cheat. On the surface the evidence is clearly against my son. I find myself wanting very much to find and believe every shred against the teacher's hypothesis. Did my son study hard for that examination? Yes. Did the boys get together and talk over the possible exam? Yes. (Good!) The teacher did not know this when she made the accusation. Did they "spot" these questions as the ones "she's sure to ask"? Yes. (Fine, fine!) Still those two papers were very similar; the boys sat next to each other; the other boy's paper seems authentic. Yet my son has never been known to cheat before, and he asks me to trust his word.

What is "the truth" in this situation? Here more than what *has taken place is in question.* More than my son's cheating or not cheating is in the crucible. In fairness to everyone it is important to know if my son has been cheating. Yet he is asking for a vote of confidence, and the evidence is not "without doubt" against him. What will happen if, in view of a clean past record, the teacher and even his father do not give him the benefit of the doubt? He may, especially at this age, when "loyalty means so much," when he may not yet have developed the capacity to withstand such a bad blow, lose his faith in his father's willingness to help him. It occurs to us that even if he did cheat this time, our faith in him in view of the inconclusiveness of the evidence, will help him to see how important it is for him not to cheat.

In a case like this, there clearly is a temptation to maximize one part of the situation and minimize another. I also want to be fair to the teacher and to the school system. Am I so anxious to be fair to others that I become unfair to one for whom I have a peculiar responsibility? I look for evidence that would clinch the case. There is none short of a confession of guilt by my son. I finally decide that, once the situation has been thoroughly examined, "the truth is" that my son did not cheat.

Here our present decision, if in his favor, may contribute to what may be the desirable situation tomorrow—a boy firmly determined to keep away from even the appearance of cheating! But it is still possible that he did cheat! Suppose he gets by this time, will it strengthen in him tendencies to cheat? Yet is it reasonable to let the negative possibilities in this case cast too much of a shadow upon our affirmative decision?

But take another situation. This time my son is seriously ill, and the family doctor says that he may die unless very difficult surgery is attempted.

How do we come to a decision in such a situation? We call in experts who confirm the family doctor's diagnosis. We check what we know over and over again. It still comes out the same way. My son *may* live without the operation. Why chance his death with a risky operation? Yet the operation may succeed. If we only knew the truth! But the truth here is not something passively accessible, "something there," for us to find. We make what seems securely hidden in the situation "come true" by our decision. Without a commitment of ourselves to what we believe is more likely, we shall not discover what the real situation is.

In this instance, as in the instance of the cheating, we might well have said that what we do is *a matter of faith!* But it is very important to realize what we mean by this *faith.* What we seem to do is to *make a decision to live by, to commit ourselves, on the basis of the best evidence at our disposal* (*not without evidence*). Our commitment is based on less than complete evidence, but follows the trend of the evidence that would lead to desired results. The decision is coherent with the evidence at hand, but it still might be the wrong one. Yet to wait is to gain no advantage and may hurt the chance of success in the operation. So what we do is to risk the boy's life—for he might survive without an operation—on an operation that if successful will bring him back to health. This is "reason grown courageous," or *reasonable faith,* or *being reasonable*—in short, it is using *growing coherence* as a test for truth.

We could still be deceived in such "matters of faith." Perhaps the difference between reasonable and unreasonable faith can come out in a third example. A son, let us say, has had a bad medical history in which he has been known to have accidents that endangered both himself and others. This is part of the reason for his having a borderline scholastic record. This record will not by itself keep him out of college. Yet if the college authorities know about this medical history they will not take him.

As the father confronts the college questionnaire asking about his son's health, what should he do? He realizes that if the boy is given another chance, in a new situation, he may improve both his scholastic and medical record. The doctors have indicated that this could happen. But the evidence points in no clear direction.

On the one side, then, new friends, new opportunity, new atmosphere, possible physical improvement, and a better scholastic record. Yet, on the other side, if the son fails, he will hurt himself and others, and find himself out of college. If the father decides to "will to believe," to "have faith," and sends in the questionnaire without any word about the boy's illness, would he not be acting in bad faith, both intellectually and morally (even apart from lying)? Was there enough evidence to warrant this step, even if committing oneself to it might turn out right?

Reasonable Faith

The argument so far is intended to show that (1) we don't just "find the truth," (2) often our own well-being is involved in trying to discover what the truth is, and (3) in such important situations we must act so as to "make the truth," that is, make the hypothesis we prefer "come true." One more illustration, similar in some respects to the one just used, may bring out clearly the nature of reasonable commitment or *reasonable faith.*

A very bright young man from a well-to-do family entered an outstanding university away from home. He had been brought up in a very strict, unreasoning religious and moral atmosphere. Every word in the Bible, he had been told, was true; certain actions were immoral beyond question. He was not to raise questions, for one should not question the authority of the Scriptures, or their interpretation by the particular Christian church to which he belonged. The intelligence of this young man had rebelled when he was in high school; yet circumstances at home were such that he was willing to conform and "not make trouble."

But when he was in a university dormitory with the other fellows his age, he felt different pressures. Many of his classmates did not agree with the views he had "accepted." They too were in the process of questioning, and they were doing things that were unthinkable for him, given his early training. His reading in literature, science, philosophy, history, and religion, let alone the lectures of his professors, brought out ideas that reinforced some of his own earlier groping. Nor did his own present desire to "find out some things for himself" decrease the emotional conflict he felt with his background and parents.

He found it impossible to work under such pressures from within and from without. His early training favored thinking in black and white; a certain belief was either clearly right or wrong. Thus, without trying to gain new perspectives on his past, he flung the teachings of his home away. As he said later, "I felt the way you do when you take off some very tight and cramping shoes—free at last!" But the consequences were to be serious.

It is one thing to throw out one's beliefs; it is another to have little else to take their place. He was still discontented, and he felt guilty, as he put it, at "going back on my folks." To shorten our story, he tried to drink away his discontent and his guilt at breaking a rigid conscience. To assert himself unmistakably in rebelling against earlier habits of religious thought and action, he went "the boys" one better in proving that he was a free man. He had rebelled in the name of truth. But he didn't seem interested even in a truth that might confirm his freedom.

Flunked out of college, he went into the armed services. The change of environment did not change his personal problem. The uniformity of action expected of him was too great. A dishonorable discharge from his country's military service landed him in New York without a resource, without a plan.

After several years of disjointed living "for the moment," he came by chance under the influence of Friends. He found much of their thought congenial and helpful. What is more, he had what he felt was an experience of the "inner light" that centered his life again, but this time not within the confines of unthinking morality. He soon was taking courses in adult education. He joined Alcoholics Anonymous, found and kept a position, began tutoring on the side, and finally decided that he wanted to go back to school and prepare himself to be a teacher.

He came for specific advice on getting back into a college where he could earn a college degree. But the colleges he was interested in were not interested in him. They had strict rules about allowing men with dishonorable discharges back into college. Without arguing the merits of the rules, we come to our problem.

Should his parents, should I and other sponsors ask that this young man be readmitted? Readmission to college might give him the very encouragement he needs to continue his improvement. The whole process might bring forth a man who, chastened by scarring experiences, has an even stronger motive to help others as a teacher. His tutoring has shown his interest and skill.

On the other side of the picture, there are long years of waywardness in his past. Competition would now be keen, and he might just not be able to discipline himself enough in study and in general behaviour. On any college campus, if he reverted to past habits, he would be a nuisance. If later, when he was a teacher, old tensions in him mounted again and he went to pieces, many families would be affected. Nevertheless, who could deny that he has an attractive personality and basic ability? In addition he has recently shown clear progress in self-possession and purposeful living.

To say that he himself should have faith in himself and in God, to say that his sponsors should join him in this faith, to say that a college should take the risk of allowing this young man back—all this is easy, until we remember what failure would mean to all concerned. Why should he not wait longer? Why not choose some other vocation? Well, he wants to teach, "to help others avoid adolescent troubles.

as he says; and the fact remains that he has been able to control himself increasingly for the past two years.

To come to the point. In this situation I am willing to have faith, a faith that does involve risks, but a faith that might "make" the very evidence we need to support the hypothesis that he can make the grade now. The important point here is that this faith is not groundless, even though there are risks. The risks are on both sides; we take a social risk by giving him a vote of confidence, but society risks losing a good man if no one is willing to trust him on the basis of his improvement and promise. Without trying to argue whether the colleges involved should break their rule, is there any real doubt as to what an advisor should recommend? For faith now means not just "commitment" but a reasonable commitment, a faith that follows the trend of the evidence.

As these examples show, wishes and wants—to believe or not to believe—cannot be left out of our daily lives as we search for truth. We seldom live by certainties. We ourselves change, situations change, and we usually cannot have the evidence we need to be as confident as we would like to be. We need *courage to become, courage to take the step which the evidence at hand makes worth taking but does not prove.*

The search for truth, in other words, is itself the search for commitment, for faith. Faith, like truth, never neglects what we know; it never runs contrary to the preponderance of evidence; it does not fly in the face of reasoned probabilities. But without commitment we cannot get on with life; commitment gives us the very opportunity we need to find out whether what we now think is so, can actually be so.

Such faith is obviously adventurous faith. But it is not something different from what we have in science. In some sciences the evidence is easier to accumulate, and the scientist is not immediately involved in the discovery hoped for. Yet even this is a matter of degree. Truth-finding is of one piece; faith is of one piece. The main difference between the truth we discover in science and the truth about God and the things that matter most to us is in the kind of commitment that our investigation requires. *We are ourselves involved* "right up to our necks" when we are seeking religious and moral truth.

Love and forgiveness, somebody says, is better than hate. But we will never know it for ourselves until we live that way. This means loving when a case could be made for hating. It means deciding to trust those who have hurt us but can now profit from our help. Again, someone may tell us that he has had an experience of the love of God, and he may give good reasons for believing in this love. But his religious faith cannot be ours until we discover it by taking every risk involved and committing our lives to it. As a matter of fact, even the scientist that walks into a laboratory to perform a crucial experiment never performed before may not escape without injury.

To summarize: There is no finding of truth-for-living without faith-for-living, or living in commitment! For we are always choosing between hypotheses, between hope and fear; human experience is so complicated and varied that there is always something that can be said in favor of almost any hypothesis. But we cannot find the truth as it applies to each of us without committing ourselves to the hypothesis that enables the facts we know, the thinking we do, *and* our acting to march hand in hand.

Again, there is no safe, neutral road to a truth for living. Whether we are choosing a college, a vocation, a mate, or a philosophy of life, we can never "know" without making our own lives laboratories where tests go on that lead to confirmation or rejection. Because we are ourselves inevitably involved, we cannot achieve the kind of objectivity possible otherwise. But there is no escape. There are truths that cost all the way because they involve beliefs about the total meaning of our lives, about the total purpose of the universe in which we live.

Thus, in the rest of this book, I am going—all too briefly—to set up certain hypotheses about God and his relation to man, and show what evidence can be correlated with them. I am not promising a mathematical demonstration, for such "proof" cannot be achieved in religion any more than it can be given in everyday life or in scientific investigation. But I shall try to show that belief in a certain conception of God is a reasonable faith-for-living. And it will be in the living that the committed person will discover whether the faith he lives by does have the promise, for himself and others, that he believes it will have.

4

What Does It Mean to Call God a Person?

In this chapter I am not trying to "prove" that God is a person. That I shall leave to the next chapter. I am hoping to make clear what has been in the minds of thinkers, especially Jewish and Christian, who have called God a person. Only when we know what we mean by calling God a person can we argue that a belief in him, a faith-for-living, is more coherent than the view that if there is a God, he is not a person.

Note how easily I have fallen into saying "he"— as if God is a man and not a woman. A Hindu I know is fond of starting his prayers with: "O Thou who art our Mother; O Thou who art our Father!" Well, do we think that God is a male or a female?

Before we answer this question, let us ask ourselves whether America is male? We refer to our country as "Uncle Sam" and to our flag as "she" or "her." Note how we shuttle back and forth in our use of "she" and "he." (Note that "she" is our motherland, but we call "her," in a different context, "Uncle Sam"! And the Statue of Liberty is a woman!)

"Person" as a Symbol

We human beings, it seems, just cannot get along without images and symbols. Symbols are short cuts; they stand for something it would take a long time to explain. "Cupid" is love; "Santa Claus" is the spirit of Christmas; and an eagle is another symbol of America! If we forget that symbols—mother or father as applied to God—are abbreviations or pointers and take them literally, we are easily misled. So, with the father symbol in mind, we are led to ask: "Does God have a white beard and a stern or benevolent look?" And when symbols are actions —like saluting the flag, tipping one's hat, shaking hands—they can become lifeless rituals. So if symbols are to fulfill their purpose, we must stop from time to time and ask what it is they are trying to suggest and bring nearer to us.

When we speak of America as our motherland, are we not trying to say that she "nurtures us" and, in the same breath, suggest tenderness? And are we not trying to encourage on our part gratitude, loyalty, and reverence, for example? What would we be without our "Mother"-land, or without our stern and yet kind "Uncle Sam"! To speak of "God" as father and mother, then, is to proclaim simply and richly, all in one, that like our earthly father and mother, God not only is the source of our being but cares for us and holds us responsible for our actions.

We have already come to a fundamental aspect of what most thinkers have in mind when they call God —some ultimate (X), without which nothing else can exist—a person. All of us believe there is this something ultimate—something which doesn't depend upon anything else for its existence, but upon which everything else in some sense depends. The next question is: What is this X like?

Most thinkers who hold that God is a person mean something like this: First, this ultimate, X, is the source of our being, more specifically, the creator and sustainer of all things. Second: X is not "something"; X is a certain kind of ultimate being. Thus, if X is a person, "he" is not, for example, to be conceived as an infinite sun which indifferently and forever sends forth heat and light rays. Nor is X an enormous reservoir of electrical energy which goes on transforming itself *unknowingly* in the billions of beings that compose the world. Third, in sum, to call God "a person" is to say that X does know and care about what is going on in the world. Things don't "just go on" in the world; nothing happens to X without X's knowing it! "He" knows and "he" cares.

To call X a person, then, is to exclude the view that we are living in a world that is "teeming with energy" but is unaware and without purpose. To call X a person is to symbolize three emphases: X is aware of what "he" is doing, cares about what "he" is doing, and is not indifferent to what goes on anywhere in the world. This may be hard to prove—and it is only a beginning of the full idea of God—but there's nothing like being aware of "which God" we have in mind. Let's take another look.

What Is a Human Person?

Calling God a person is dangerously misleading unless we are clearer about what we mean when we assign the term "person" to a human being. Note, to begin with, that every normal human being is a male or a female. But we call both males and females "persons." Why?

1. *Why aren't all living things "persons"? Why don't we call a stone or a star a person? Why don't we call a lovely plant a person?*

Plants, we say, come nearer to being human beings than stones do because plants can reproduce themselves. Animals too can reproduce. But we think of animals as closer to human beings than plants, because—especially if they are higher animals, like cats, dogs, chimpanzees—they make more complicated adjustments to their environments than do plants. The pine tree sends out shoots according to what we might call a plan. But the cat gives birth to its kittens, cuts the umbilical cord, washes and takes care of them, and seems to have a goal to reach. Still, the cat did not know "in a planning way" that she was going to have kittens. The cat does not know there will be a next week. (Obviously, we are basing what we say on reasonable hypotheses about cats.) The cat, we believe, is probably aware of doing each act as she does it, but it would be considered farfetched to say that she is aware of why she is doing it.

There is controversy as to the degree of similarity or dissimilarity there is between animals, and especially between chimpanzees, and human beings; but at the closest there is no denying a vast difference. For example, the cat and the human mother reproduce, but the human mother has been able to learn from others and her own past experience about what reproduction is and what it involves. Her baby comes to mean "life itself" to her, she may say, and she makes special plans to help that baby grow into a certain admirable kind of human being. The cat may do what is necessary for its kittens with an efficiency that may seem at times to human beings almost maternal. Yet the human mother and the mother cat seem almost similar only with respect to biological processes.

Thus we have reasons for distinguishing one kind of thing from another, a stone from a cat, a cat from a human being. If we find good reason to suppose that any two beings have something in common we put them in the same class. Stones and stars, though different, are in the class, we say, of inanimate beings. Plants and cats are in the class of reproductive living beings, but they differ from each other in that cats are more able to learn from experience and are conscious. Human beings too are conscious and able to learn from experience. But they are in a class by themselves. They alone can know what they are doing now in connection with some conscious plan for the future. They are persons, whether they are male or female.

We have come to a clearer awareness of what it means to be a (human) person by noting what we human beings have in common with, and how we differ from, animals and plants. We could say "the analogy," the proportion of similarity, is closer between chimpanzees and human beings than between chimpanzees and pine trees. When we thus try to understand something we don't know on the basis of something we know, we are reasoning by analogy.

The caution we must observe when we think by analogy is to make sure that the analogy holds. We must show that there is enough similarity between what we know and what we infer to justify the inference. Thus, from the fact that animals are male and female and reproduce as do human beings, we cannot infer that they have the capacity to think and plan that human beings have. In reasoning from human persons "down" to animals we have seen that no analogy justifies calling them persons. Now comes the question: "Are we justified in going by analogy from human persons *up* to God, the divine Person?"

2. *How safe is it to call God a person?*

A human being is a male or a female, but we are not willing to say that *a person* is a male or female, because this is not what counts about a person. If we remember this we will not be misled into thinking: "Because God is a person, 'he' is a male or a female, with a male or female body." Nor shall we say that because God is a person "he" is young or old, or white, or red, or brown! But more significantly, we cannot assume that because human persons we know have bodies like ours, there cannot be persons without bodies like ours.

Indeed, it is this conviction, that we are the persons we are because we have bodies like ours, that has led some influential philosophers and theologians to urge that it is better not to call God a person. They also fear that if we do this, people will be thinking that God has blue eyes, a flowing beard, abundant white hair, and that he sits on a throne, eats indescribable meals, and drinks nectar. And this is surely a very poor way to think of the ultimate.

To think this is to think by analogy, to be sure. But the analogy is false, because it has been sidetracked into unesssential factors. People who called God a person and said "he" and "father" *forgot the core of the symbol's meaning* and worked with the accidental details. Perhaps some people cannot think of "America" unless they are clutching the cloth of the flag, but "the stars and stripes" must not be allowed to bury the inner meaning of America.

We can in fact say that, as used for God, the divine Person, the symbol "person" philosophically never was restricted to "having a body" any more than having a human body was restricted to having a beard or blue eyes. In any case, the essential factor about a person is that "he" is the kind of being that can be aware that he is aware (be self-aware, or self-conscious). A person can think, can have plans or ideals, and can direct his actions by those plans (can care).

But another crucial point remains. A human person is always a unity of thinking, feeling, willing, at least. He is not a mere combination of separate capacities; you can't make him by sticking together thinking, willing, and feeling. He must be *a unity to begin with,* whose very nature it is to think, will, and feel.*

A person, then, at the human level is the kind of unified self-conscious being who can think (know), feel (care), and will (create or execute with some degree of freedom), in accordance with some ideal or purpose. If we should get to another planet and find creatures with an anatomy quite different from ours but who could do mathematics, teach each other, live according to some ideal, we should have to call them persons. If we can show that there is a unified, self-conscious X who can know, care, and will, we shall have reasonable ground for considering this being a person, without saying that in every respect X is like the finite (human) person.

---

* I would want to spell this out further and say that a person is a complex unity of sensing, remembering, perceiving, thinking, imagining, feeling, emoting, willing, and oughting; but some of this would be quite controversial, and it is not necessary for our main point.

What Is a Divine Person?

To call God "a person," then, is to say that X is a being who is a unity that knows what is going on in himself and in the universe that depends upon him, who acts in accordance with ideals, and cares about what happens enough to control his ways in accordance with his ideals.

Here again, however, we must interpret our meaning with due regard for the dangers in thinking by analogy. When we use the words "knows," "acts," and "does," we are no more insisting that he knows in the same way that we do than we are insisting that his "language" is English, or that he has will and feelings exactly like ours. Our analogy would run away with us again, as it does with those who connect God with a male or female body. We mean simply that what God undergoes when he knows, acts, and feels is such that, granted the enormous differences in degree that must be allowed for between self-sufficient X and puny creatures like us, he is better called a person than an animal or a thing—or, as we shall see, a non-personal One. "Person" makes a better analogy—better than any other we can think of—but we must go on to make proper allowances for differences "upwards" as we did for animals and plants "downwards."

Man may thus be considered made in the "image of God" in the language of Genesis 2. Some think it smart to say that man returns the compliment and makes God in his own image when he calls him a person. But would such people seriously prefer to liken God to an unknowing something "lower down" than man, such as the sun, or to a great reservoir of energy? They too, incidentally, are using analogy in referring to God, for the images they contrive are drawn from what we are acquainted with in our world. Is it not more worthy of God to speak of him in terms of "he" rather than in terms of "it"?

Others somehow think to do more honor to God by saying that God is a being "beyond all our knowledge." He is more, no doubt, than the best we can think even when we think of a mind that is the source and sustainer of our whole cosmos. But can that "more" mean that he does not know himself and his creation, and act forever with them in mind? This is why we must say: not "more than we can know," but "Knower-Creator Person at the core of whatever else X is." What would "more than we can know" mean, if taken seriously? How do we know such a being isn't an oblong blur?

Wholly Other

What these people probably have in mind is that nothing we say will be adequate. This is readily admitted. But can we thus avoid the responsibility for the best symbol our knowledge allows? The most we are saying in calling God a person is that he is continuous with the best kind of being we know, and—without false humility—that is a person.

We do better, therefore, to take a cue from the writer of the first chapter of Genesis. God, he says, after having created the order of the world and the animals, used a model when he made man. God made man in his own image. Why did this writer say this? Did he realize that, unlike any thing or animal, man is a thinker, a planner, a purposer? Was it that he meant to bring the creator of the heavens and the earth closer to man? No, a being like man, he speculated, must be nearer to an infinite person than to animals or plants. Thus, he said, man was made "in the image of God," the universe-planner and creator.

We have already warned that when we think by analogy we can easily be led astray. For example, if I meet another human being who speaks my language and enjoys the kinds of tales I do, I am tempted to think that he likes to play tennis as I do— and cannot do mathematics either! We have already seen how many mistakes we can make if we allow talk about God as "he" or "father" to allow us to think of X as being male, white-bearded, white-skinned, and English-speaking. Believers in a personal God have often been chided for being "anthropomorphic," that is, for turning God into man. They deserve such criticism when they use analogy carelessly. But to be forewarned is to be forearmed.

Our human situation in knowing "what God is like" can be better understood, I suggest, if we think of it in this way. Men have always been, and are, enshrouded in mystery. The universe we live in will always be beyond the reach of even our best knowledge. Yet we want to know, we want to grasp with our minds, the mysterious X that is reality. Our only way to do so is to think of X as "like this" or "like that," some model our minds can firmly grasp as a basis for further imagination and thought.

Note, for example, how physicists and chemists try to help themselves work with their microscopic world by building imaginary models of molecules and even atoms. The question for the physicist in his restricted world, and for us all when we face the mystery of X, is: What model of it seems to do most justice to the facts we know? Is it more coherent to say that X is a person—a self-conscious unity of knowing, feeling, and acting—than to say that X does not know, care, and act? With this personalistic view, the Judeo-Christian tradition has mainly agreed; but it has added other meanings also to the statement that God is a person, which we must now consider.

What Kind of Person Is God?

Each person is not simply a unity of knowing, caring, acting. As an individual person he is a kind of person. God, by analogy, is a person with certain qualities, and they make him worthy of men's reverence and worship. Traditional Jewish, Christian, and Moslem personalists* have been anxious to allow

* In each tradition there are good thinkers who conceived of God as one, and superpersonal. The word "personalist" or "theist" will be used interchangeably for the view that God is a person, creator of, but not one with, the world and men (see Chapter 7).

for the vast difference they felt must exist between the Person on whom all depends and the "spark" of the divine in human persons. To express this difference they urged that God is all-powerful (omnipotent), that he is all-knowing (omniscient), and that he is all-good (morally perfect).

To put the difference in other terms: We are dependent on God, but God is self-sufficient. We know in part and bit by bit, but God knows all and all at once. We strive to perfect our natures by loving; but God loves from the very perfection of his being.

In the Judeo-Christian view the emphasis is uniquely placed on God's loving us so much that he deals with us not in accordance with our desert, but beyond anything we could ever deserve. He is a judge who does not sentence us according to our behavior; he is not interested in a justice that distributes merits and demerits as such. He is a father who, in forgiving love, is interested in bringing us back into the family of love, into a responsible fellowship with him and with all of his children.

There is a beautiful myth by which believers in the Judeo-Christian tradition like to express the basic relation they believe exists between themselves and God. "Myth" does not mean a false story, but a story that tells symbolically about a mystery. It is not history, but a way of bringing out dramatically what "the facts" mean. Thus, in Genesis 1:3 God created Adam and Eve in a world in which they could be free to rule under God. We interpret the story to mean that God does not make it impossible for any man (Adam) to disobey him; He trusts him and prefers to leave it up to man to respect the relationship of trust between him and his maker. But man disobeys and breaks the relationship of trust. This fact of life, which each of us exemplifies in his own life, the Bible pictures in the scene of Adam's disobedience and of his expulsion with Eve from the close and harmonious fellowship of love between man and God in the Garden of Eden.

For the Christian theist, who sees all this through the eyes of Jesus, the meaning of the Old Testament "myth" of man's disobedience is given a new dimension in the light of later events. The Genesis account suggests that God punished Adam and Eve, as a stern parent would, and drove them out of the fellowship with him in the Garden. Seen through what Jesus tells us of God, this act of expulsion marked only the end of one kind of relationship. Now begins God's suffering love, revealed by the very fact that he made man so that obedience or disobedience was up to each man. God never gives up trying to save men from their willful selves. He won't force them to obey or to repent, but he rejoices when they come back to him.

Jesus spoke of this relation in the touching parable of the Prodigal Son (Luke 15). The father in this parable gives by request to his willful son his share of his inheritance. The son leaves home and before long has beggared himself with riotous living. When he decides to return home, he finds his father eagerly awaiting him, and ordering a feast to celebrate the return of the son who was once lost and is now found.

The person God, as Jesus saw him in this parable, is a loving father who will not allow his children to suffer more than they must when they break the laws of loving trust. He is willing to forgive his children—finite persons who can think, care, and act—even when they abuse their freedom. And he is willing to go on giving of himself in order that they may understand that only through responsible love and responsible freedom can the greatest good be realized in God's world.

Christians believe different things about Jesus in his relation to God. I do not suggest that what I am about to say is a full or adequate account. But in Jesus' life, teaching, death, and resurrection, Christians believe they see God at work trying to show men what it means to live in God's world. More specifically, in the Jesus who yielded himself so completely to the God of compassion and forgiving love, who sought to see God's vision of each person he met, who treated others as God's children, and who was willing to die on a cross, an innocent victim of the misguided wrath of his fellow men—in this Jesus, Christians believe they see what God has always done, and forever will do, with men and for men. And the main Christian tradition has insisted that in Jesus—the Son of God and the son of man—

God was at work and is at work reaching to bring every man into the fellowship of his love.

Again I am not here trying to give a final view of Jesus, but to suggest in minimal terms what it means in one great human tradition to say that God is not only a person, but a loving person. Does this kind of God provide a reasonable faith-for-living? Or is this belief, in which so much of our Western civilization especially is rooted, a wish without substance? We shall begin in the next chapter to draw up a line of approach to an answer.

5

Can Faith in God
Follow from Faith in Science?

Each of us lives by a fundamental faith that undergirds everything else we do. We take it for granted, as we do the air we breathe. What is that faith? It is the faith that our minds can know the world. We make all kinds of mistakes, of course. But if we couldn't correct any of them, we couldn't know they are mistakes.

We must take a good look at this amazing fact. It is so easy to mock human reason and talk about taking too much pride in it. And it is unfortunate that often religious people are in the front ranks of those who throw stones at reason. What we shall try to show is that trust in reason, including scientific reasoning, far from leading away from God, takes us toward the personal God we have been describing. In this chapter we shall see that hidden away in the scientific dependence on experimental reason is good evidence for belief in a cosmic intelligence.

Why Is Human Knowing Trustworthy?

Your mind did not make my mind. Yet despite
our misunderstandings, how does it happen that we
can communicate with and know each other? Why
should any two minds, let alone millions of minds,
be able to understand each other and check on each
other's mistakes? If minds could not communicate
with each other, there would be no social life. Nor
would there be any science. For science, after all,
is human beings communicating with each other
as they methodically put certain questions to nature.

This capacity to "communicate"—without it no
art, no science, no morality, no religion, no *human*
daily life is possible—depends on the fact that our
minds can be orderly in the same way in an orderly
world. We would not try to communicate if we
could not have reasonable faith that despite differences between people, and other difficulties in
people and the world, we are parts of a more dependable order of things than the one we ourselves
make. We must look at this matter more closely.

Your mind and my mind did not make our bodies,
did not make the regularities of bodily growth, fa-
tigue, and decay. Nor did they make the world of
plants and animals from which we choose what
vegetables, fish, and meat we can use to nourish our
bodies. Over the years our human minds have had
to learn about this whole biological world of plants
and animals, including knowledge of what parts of

the animal and plant world our bodies can digest with profit. Now, since our minds did not make the plant and animal world, we ask: How does it happen anyway that we can actually come to understand what we did not create but is still so vital to us? Indeed, how does it happen that we have the kinds of minds and bodies able to survive in this world that they did not create?

Suppose, for a moment, that these laws of biology and physiology should change radically. Suppose that carrots developed hidden poisons our minds could not fathom, and that this happened with all vegetables, fish, and meat. Who would remain alive to tell the tale?

Let me repeat, this fundamental fact that what goes on in our minds—when we sense, remember, perceive, imagine, think—can correspond with what goes on in a world they did not make, is a fact we take completely for granted. We are even surprised and taken aback when we make mistakes. Often, without realizing it, we behave like little children who have become so accustomed to mother's dependability and goodness that they are surprised, even resentful, when mother withholds her kindness until they obey and meet the requirements of comradeship. This world we live in might have been so made that we, its children, with our particular minds and bodies, could not manage knowing and surviving. Because we can and do adjust in body and mind to our world, we cease to wonder that it should be so, and not otherwise.

But even the fact that we do take our world for granted has its lesson. We take for granted that we can know *only if we already believe that things are so organized that we can know and survive in that world if we discipline our minds and our bodies.* Nature seems to be like a teacher who not only suggests questions to be asked but answers questions we put to her in the right spirit and with the determination to know. Nature responds to disciplined intelligence.

But is this by pure accident? I immediately admit that it could be. We have agreed that no mathematical demonstration is possible of belief in God, or of most other beliefs. But what is this pure accident? Is it reasonable to believe in pure accident?

Imagine a field in which we see thousands of colored bricks such as those used for building. No two are of exactly the same color, but they all are rectangular in shape and do not differ much in size. But suppose we also see that all those bricks are in groups of three, two upright and a third bridging them. Would we say that these many similar combinations occurred by pure accident, or would we look further for some underlying cause or purpose for this particular arrangement?

Everywhere else, when we see basic harmonies, we don't try to account for them by "pure accident." Why should we when it comes to this most amazing "arrangement" of minds and bodies in the field they exist in? In order to explain this arrangement, isn't it a more reasonable hypothesis that our minds, properly disciplined, can know each other and nature because they were framed by a cosmic mind (to some extent at least like ours)? If finite persons can know nature as they work with it, may it not be because there is a cosmic person, not unlike them in basic structure, at work in nature?

Can't "Evolution" Better Explain Our Success in Knowing?

"But," some readers will say, "you forget evolution." In the course of history, plants and animals survive only if they can adapt themselves to their environment. It happens that our minds and bodies have been able to survive because they could adapt themselves so ingeniously to many changing conditions in their environment. Why not explain our mind's ability to know nature in this way?

On this "evolutionary view" our mind can know nature, then, not because of some divine plan or purpose. Over the millions of years in which living beings have been developing, our kinds of minds turned out to be the only species that survived the challenges of nature. Nature didn't ask for us, or protect us in some motherly way. We were not among the creatures who failed to meet or adapt themselves to nature's conditions and therefore fell to the side.

Our human minds, in a word, did meet the require-

ments for "the survival of the fit," so here we are—
surviving! We weren't put in a world "made for us
to survive," but in a world that would have eliminated us too as it eliminated many other species. So
on this view, given millions of kinds of plants and
animals and millions of years for changes that favored some and destroyed others, in time, by chance
—yes by "pure accident"—why couldn't creatures like
men develop and survive? Why call in some God, or
divine plan, to explain what we can explain so
naturally" rather than "supernaturally"?

But this objection, often advanced, misses the point
of my argument. *It explains the survival of the fit
but not the arrival of those that could fit.* Why, in
a world in which there is supposed to be no Intelligence; why, in a world that for millions of years
had no minds like ours—why should minds like
ours appear? Our kinds of minds did arrive! And
they did survive! This is a fact. More than that, it
is a fact about our world. Why make the fact that
mind arrived and survived so hard to explain by
saying: "There is no basis for mind in the universe.
It just arrived, that's all, and managed to survive."
If we do so, aren't we going in for mysteries instead
of reasons?

We agreed, on the contrary, to commit ourselves
to a hypothesis as true, as part of our reasonable
faith-for-living, if it accounted for the facts at our
disposal better than any other. The facts should not
be forced to fit the hypothesis; the hypothesis should

be changed to fit the facts. What, then, are the basic facts to be kept in mind?

Minds like ours came into existence with bodies like ours after millions of years, when, so far as we know, there were no such minds. There may be other minds, with bodies like or unlike ours, on other planets; but if there are, it would certainly not weaken our hypothesis. Minds like ours did appear, and over the years they found that their logic and mathematics, their scientific method and reasonableness were applicable to their environment. Human minds could and did manage to stay alive by assuming that they "fit" nature in such a way that they could plumb nature's deepest secrets, fathom its probable past and predict its probable future.

Does it, then, really make more sense to say that the appearance of such minds, and their ability to know the environment into which they are born and by which they are sustained, is happenstance? Since we have assumed, and confirmed, this general correspondence between the world we live in and our mind's best efforts, does it not make more sense to call the world, not mindless, but mind-full?

Scientific minds thrive on plan, order, exactness. Is it "science" that forces us to see these scientific minds as lucky accidents in a world that, even more fortunately, could welcome this kind of accident? Surely this is straining toward disbelief. If we can trust our understanding of evolution, why not trust the universe which made it possible for minds to be fit and discover evolution?

The Faith Scientists Live By

We must fill in the bare skeleton of thinking about science and cosmic intelligence that has been advanced. Indeed, the argument has already pushed beyond certain details of which we must be aware.

First, we need to be reminded that there is no such thing as "science," just as there is no such thing as "religion." There are only men dedicated to the discovery of truth in accordance with scientific method. These men are inspired by the scientific spirit, the willingness to follow the lines of evidence wherever they may lead. The scientific *method* and the scientific *spirit* unite men of science from many different fields into a "scientific community," as we often call it. But there is no science over and above men.

There are also men dedicated to the discovery of God and to the meaning of God in their lives—"the religious community," we call it. These minds too are inspired by the religious *spirit*—a spirit so beautifully expressed in the words of Jesus, "Not my will, but thine." However, the religious *spirit*—of reverence for God, of obedience to his will—does not have *a particular method*, like the scientific method, by which all religious persons are guided in finding God.

There are other differences too, on which I must

not dwell; yet they are not so great as to overshadow certain suggestive similarities common to the scientific spirit and the religious spirit.

First, neither is self-centered; both have an object, or objective—truth and God respectively.

Second, neither can seek its objective without self-discipline.

Third, both are willing to move by faith, faith supported by the private experience of individuals and the discoveries of groups. Scientists and religious men grow in communities that nourish them, even though individuals often, and without being appreciated, go further than their "community" will go.

Fourth—and this is what our discussion has been pointing toward—there is an underlying faith by which the scientist lives, although he may not call it faith. It is the faith in the "uniformity of nature." And it is a faith that is better justified if we can think of it as being part of the faith that there is a cosmic person or mind. What exactly is this faith in the "uniformity of nature"?

When you press your foot on the gas accelerator of your car you expect the car to speed up. Why? Because you believe that the gas will be ignited and the explosion in the engine will, by a series of steps, accelerate the car. But why do you believe that what happened to the gas yesterday will also happen today? This explosion does not follow as necessarily as two plus two equals four. Your belief is in the "uniformity of nature." You are trusting nature to "keep its word," as it were. If gas, given certain conditions, ignited yesterday, it will ignite today and tomorrow.

We all live by this faith in the uniformity of nature —that the conditions (A B) which caused C to happen yesterday in Boston will cause C to happen anywhere else (if the conditions are the same).

The scientist lives his life as a scientist on this faith. He walks into the laboratory, sets up his experiments, and expects the "laws of nature" to go on operating as they have. Suppose a given experiment does not succeed. He does not blame "the disorderly universe." He blames himself. If he must take the blame, it is because he cannot but trust the "laws of nature," or more generally, the uniformity of nature. (If only more people whose prayer to God is unfulfilled were ready to assume that it must have been the wrong prayer!)

To be specific, some early workers with radium found the flesh dropping off their bones. They had not discovered yet the precautions to take. They did not blame a disorderly nature. They and their colleagues who succeeded them assumed a dependable order as they tried to correct their mistakes.

We cannot say it soberly enough: scientific men have been the saints or heroes of many ventures in knowledge. But would they have become heroes if they had not had their own faith-for-living in the uniformity of nature? But actually this uniformity of nature is only another way of saying that scientists believe they can trust their minds and the hypotheses they make *in this kind of a world.*

What kind of world must this be? One in which their minds are lucky aliens, or foreign prospectors, just happening to strike it lucky? Or is the world one which is expressing the will of a cosmic mind who, by keeping nature orderly, enables minds like ours to learn how to proceed in the effort to know more, and live better, in the uniformity he has ordained?

We cannot make enough of this hidden faith by which we and all scientists in fact do live. The human mind, when it disciplines itself, when it is not illogical, when it bases its theories on careful observation, when it sets up its observations and experiments cautiously but courageously, can throw back the frontiers of darkness. Why? *Because what is now unknown to its mind is not unknowable.* And why is this? Because in nature there is another mind at work, co-operating with our own minds. When we believe, as we do, that where there is a jungle of ignorance we can press on with our tools and build the city of knowledge, we are believing that our minds and "what is" are not really strangers. Any given jungle is no more a jungle in principle than those which our minds have turned into ordered cities.

Which God Supports Scientific Faith?

Is there "a moral" to draw from this view of the scientific faith-for-living? Science, as we usually think of it, does not "prove" that there is a God. But the uniformity of nature—a neutral description—is what matters most to the scientist. This "steadiness" of nature is the source of his strength; it is his "God." The only God the scientist *as scientist* cannot live by is a God who is disorderly, who co-operates by whims and not by long-run plans. For the scientist, any God that is to be consistent with his "faith and finding" cannot be illogical, planless, disorderly.

God is still God, call him by whatever name. That is, a cosmic mind is still a cosmic mind even though it is called the "uniformity of nature" or, more simply, the "order of nature." Just as religious people do not go about murmuring the name of God, but gradually find that they are moulding their lives around their belief, so the scientist does not go around reciting to himself the creed: "I believe that my mind, on the basis of what I know, can move into the unknown" or, "I believe in the "uniformity of nature." He lives in that faith and lives that faith. Only on special, very risky occasions does he probably come to full consciousness of how much he depends upon it.

Thus it takes an adventure in scientific discovery, like the voyages in orbit around the earth of the Russian and American astronauts, to sting us into the realization of how much we depend on "the trustworthiness of things." Our astronauts literally took their laboratories into space with them. And their own lives constituted part of the experiment. With them in their capsules in space, hundreds of their scientific colleagues on earth were putting into practice all that physicists, chemists, biologists, and other scientists believed to be true about their bodies under those conditions unknown to man thus far. The almost infinite detail of mathematics, physics, chemistry, biology, and psychology known to men had been co-ordinated with each other and the human factor. The capsules and their complicated network of instruments had been adjusted to the atmosphere and other conditions in space. Thousands of "uniformities" in nature, dependent on fundamental "uniformities" between men's minds and between the human mind and nature, were being put to the test. There must be no mistake.

Thus in our first astronauts' flights we have most dramatic examples of the scientists' faith that what they already know, their calculations and their engineering know-how, will stand them in good stead even in relatively unchartered areas and atmospheres of outer space. What "must be right" in intricate human reckonings here below must also "work out right" out there. A John Glenn, trained in body, mind, and spirit, is chosen to put this gigantic faith in "scientific probability" into action. Well could the people of the world stand still and wait in suspense as these astronauts bet their lives that the universe is governed everywhere by the same basic physical laws.

The undaunted courage involved in these flights

might well captivate the ordinary spectator and the expert. But the stakes were even higher for the philosophical mind: nothing less than the grand bet that the laws that operate in outer space were the same as those their minds had discovered in known space. In the words of Addison's hymn one could sing of movements there in space as of movements here: "In reason's ear they all rejoice," and "the hand that made us is divine."

The astronauts' was not blind faith; it was scientific reason grown courageous. And this scientific, reasonable faith was rooted, when we come down to it, in a broader faith. What is it? *That man, the active knower, does not live in a world hostile to his disciplined efforts. That man, man courageous and disciplined, man helpful and co-operative, can be at home in this world together with the children of his mind and brain.*

But again, man as scientist learns much as he goes along. The *God of man as scientist* is not a God who works by suspending the laws of man and nature as he has ordained them. He is the God who silently and faithfully keeps the machinery of things going in such a way that men can run the machine, within limits, once they come to respect it for its own sake and understand it.

When John Glenn was asked whether his belief in God helped him when he was in the capsule, there was a quiet eloquence in his reply that he had made his peace with God long before his flight. He had dedicated his life, we might say, to the investigation of what he believed true and disciplined men could discover in a world whose order could be trusted.

Glenn's God, we might say, did not "show off" by special miracles. For a special miracle involving Glenn would not help Scott Carpenter prepare for his flight. Indeed, if Glenn's flight had been such that men would have had to attribute its success at some point to miracle rather than to law, Scott Carpenter's "count down" might not yet have occurred. For just that miracle would have thrown the investigators into confusion. The element of miracle would have introduced the element of chance and would have thrown doubt upon the uniformity of law. God was being trusted all the way—to keep the order of the universe steady for Glenn, Carpenter, and all who might follow them and learn from their experience.

Such a God is not an absentee landlord, or a watch-maker who makes the watch and lets it run. But neither does he adjust the watch to men's time just because they fail to observe. He—if we need an image—is the master engineer who sees to it that the machinery keeps running in a pattern that makes it possible for men to know its nature and to predict with dependable accuracy how it will run. God's co-engineers, however, must accept the responsibility for study and training. Then they must be willing to bet their lives that their minds, disciplined and courageously used, have not been strangers or aliens in the universe, that what seems "right" to the human brain "in here" is "right" for the universe "out there."

The cosmic Person, then, can be declared dependable and good to man as scientist. Can he be considered good to man as a total person?

6

Is God Good?

We have been suggesting that the scientist's faith-for-living, when followed back to its assumptions, leads us to the reasonable belief that nature's schedule is the working of a cosmic person. Scientific method is an ideal of investigation that has been hammered out in a world that decrees: "Discover the order of nature or perish." The conditions for scientific discovery, therefore, take us a good way toward discovering "which God" we can believe in when it comes to learning the truth about nature. How can we learn the truth concerning goodness?

When we asked the question, "Is God a person?" we realized that before we could answer, we needed more than a naïve and uncritical view of what "person" means. Now we confront the same situation when we ask: "Is God good?" Until we can decide what could make either God or man good, we shall continue to waver in our thinking about "which God."

Good—for Fulfillment

We shall never even get off the ground in our search for the "goodness" of God if we simply list all the goods or values (or evils and disvalues) in the roster of human experience. So I shall attempt a breakthrough by asking: What are the goods or values without which all other values would be impossible? But I must first start by suggesting what I believe it means to say, "God is good."

God is good, I propose, *in the sense that he is the ultimate source and constant support of the growth of persons.*

I shall go about defending this statement in a way that many thinkers would say is the wrong way. They would not agree with me that we should answer the question: Is God good? in the same way that we answer the question: Is mother good? We decide whether mother is good or bad through her relation to what we think is good for us. And certainly each of us, since his infancy, has had many second thoughts in this matter. As children we believed that it was good for us to have what we wanted when we wanted it. In those years we thought mother was "mean" when she did not give us what we wanted. With the years we have learned better as individuals—and so has the human race.

I am suggesting, then, that in our calmer and wiser moments the answer we would give to the question: When is mother good to us? is this: Mother is good to us if mother acts in such a way that she encourages and supports our attempts to grow as persons, that is, to fulfill our natures as persons. And this I believe is the same *general* answer that most thinking persons have given, although not in these words.

This general answer simply says that to grow is always more important than to get "what I want when I want it." This general answer also means that whatever will bring out, or fulfill, the best in each of us, is what we shall consider good, or most valuable. A general answer is too abstract, so I shall give it body by a description of "good" in three steps.

1. Good—for truth-finding?

Fortunately, the first step in our inquiry about what helps us to fulfill our natures takes us back over familiar ground. We have seen that we are thinking beings who need to know what kind of a world we are living in. But can we fulfill our natures as thinking beings unless we live in an environment that answers our reasonable questions? If God is to be good to us, then he must not frustrate our disciplined attempts to find the truth.

But if our conclusions in the last chapter are at all correct, our world behaves as a good God in this sense would behave. If we put logical questions to nature, if we collect the evidence our senses bring us, if we correlate the evidence with hypotheses as reasonably as possible, if we take action, even heroic action, that is consistent with our hypotheses (as did the astronauts), what do we find? We find that nature, far from going back on us, not only supports us but also challenges us to further exploration.

But again, as we have already seen, our human race did not just snatch the principles of good investigation out of the air. We did not make the world. We were brought forth in it and we found in ourselves what had been implanted there: the basic capacity to think. We have had to learn what goodness in thinking is, and that goodness is more than intellectual. What does this mean?

Our race has discovered that the world we live in does not encourage intellectual laziness, carelessness, and lack of imagination. As the history of human scientific investigation shows, nature says to us —Think hard (don't give up before knotty problems)! Think broadly (keep your mind on the whole horizon of human experience and knowledge)! Think deeply (don't assume that what you can't see on the surface is not there)!

Thinking isn't the only value, to be sure, but ask yourself: Have I ever (has the human race ever) lost anything because of hard, broad, and deep thinking?

This is not all. We seldom stop to count our blessings, but when we do we realize that *nothing else that is good for human beings would be possible were it not for our capacity to know, to be thoughtful!* Every other "good" experience, from health through love to beauty, to religious devotion, is possible to us because we are thinking beings.

If tempted to doubt this, consider the idiot child. He may be physically healthy; the senses by which he takes in his environment—such as touch, taste, smell—may be in good order. But because he has no intelligence, because he cannot think, he cannot *know what sense impressions mean,* or use them as clues to much else. How limited his enjoyments are! Who would want to change places with him?

Go a step further, then. Suppose God had stopped with the higher animals and not created Adam and Eve, who could "wonder about things," who could even disobey him. Would God's world in fact be as rich without Adam and Eve? It would remain full of forms and possibilities of experience, but with no human minds to pick and choose and enjoy them. I doubt that the answer can be affirmative.. Yet, if God, having made Adam and Eve thinking beings, eager to understand a world that seemed to promise lawful behavior, had then allowed the world to be undependable and unlawful, would we call him good? Hardly.

Straight thinking and comprehensive thinking (including scientific thinking) is not only something we enjoy for itself. It is also the condition for all the other goods we have. A God who made thinking beings possible and provided a world that would challenge and support the growth of thinking, is to be considered good. Indeed, if we follow our evidence, God seems to be using the world in order to say to us: "You cannot be fully human, you cannot get the most out of yourselves or the world, if you do not think—hard, broad, and deep. I am God, and good, because I have created and do maintain the conditions for such thought." Here, then, is the first step in the answer to the question: Is God good?

Good enough to account for the obstacles to growth?
But an important objection must be met. A reader might well say: "This world does not make it so easy as you seem to think even for hard-thinking and acute minds. Our best minds in science, for example, encounter tremendous problems in scientific research, problems that lead to no end of frustration for thinkers, and to many evils for all mankind. Because our best thinkers cannot solve far-reaching physical, biological, and psychological problems, we still have typhoons, we still have cancer and heart disease and hundreds of unsolved health problems—not to mention psychological and social problems. It almost seems as though, far from having the unqualified support of the universe in his thinking, man is constantly running aground on shoals of opposition. He seems to have to wrest the truth from nature. How do you account for such great difficulties, for such an excess of evil?"

I believe that problems raised by objections like these, taken together with others, must be faced squarely. When they are, I believe that God will best be conceived as himself changing in some respects as he seeks to improve all the conditions for goodness in the world.* Such a God, limited in power but unlimited in goodness, does not have the support of most great thinkers, and it certainly is not the main Judeo-Christian tradition; yet I believe a good case may be made for a finite-infinite God.

I do not develop the case here because, space limitations aside, the main issue is whether the problem of evil is solved by denying the existence of a personal God. The evil in the world is not so evil as to justify reasonable faith in the non-existence of God. On the other hand, the evil in the world is so evil that I am not satisfied with traditional argument for a good God who is all-powerful.

However, whatever the final solution to the problem of excess evil is, must we not admit this much? Our advances in solving even seemingly insoluble problems are tremendous. We certainly cannot say on the basis of this evidence that God doesn't care for our intellectual success, or that he is opposed to our development. It just doesn't look as though we were fighting *a concerted opposition or a blind indifference.*

The obstacles, I grant, are big enough so that, again, from where we sit it is always possible to argue that God doesn't care. But one question will not down.

* The problem of what is called technically "a finite-infinite God" involves advanced speculation. It is treated in an elementary way in my *Introduction to the Philosophy of Religion* (New York: Prentice Hall, 1951) and *Religion as Creative Insecurity* (New York: Association Press, 1954).

Why did minds like ours appear at all in a world that, despite pockets of resistance, still keeps on responding to our best intellectual efforts? The most reasonable answer still seems to me: There is a ruling mind that is interested in giving thinking beings a world in which they can think with profit, if not always with adequate success. This conclusion is supported by the thought that if God had positive ill-will, or even the ill-will of indifference toward thinking beings, man would never have come in knowledge, and with all that depends on knowledge, as far as man has come.

Yet, why have we not done more with what we have? Why have we failed to succeed in intellectual enterprises? The answer takes us from intellectual values to ethical values and shows how they are related. For we, in our societies, are likely to be casual about our efforts in understanding and in promoting the development of understanding and thinking. Not only do we not honor intellectual ability and effort enough, but we give them skimpy support. Our best thinkers have had often to combat prejudices of their fellow men who did not like some of their discoveries, whether in astronomy or physics, biology or psychology—think of Galileo, Copernicus, Darwin, and Freud. Were it not for the courage, patience, and honesty of such men, and were it not for the support lent by some of their fellow men in the midst of persecution, society would have benefited even less than it has from their contributions to its welfare and fulfillment.

Thus the intellectual life cannot develop by itself. It depends upon the good will both of the individual and his community. It does not live in a vacuum. It thrives only in a person who is morally developed to the point of daring to seek the truth wherever it may be found, despite natural obstacles and social disapproval. Every new truth has its enemies, and the truth-finder needs to live for more than prestige and economic gain, or even recognition in his time. But the society that would benefit by truth must seek ever to improve the conditions for truth-finding. In this fact, again, God seems to be saying: "In the kind of world that I have established, the search for truth requires not only thinking ability but moral courage, honesty, and co-operation among men. There can be no knowledge or increase of truth without character or the growth of character in individual men and in society."

2. Good—for character?

Thus without thinking aimed at truth, every other good in human life is endangered. But thought, and every good springing from it, depend upon intellectual self-discipline. This is the self-discipline of loyalty to the right or the good as we see it. This willingness to discipline oneself for what one believes to be right and good, is called *character*. Since truth-finding fails

where character is weak, I shall argue that character
is a condition of human growth.

We can realize how important character is for
human fulfillment if we think, as we did with regard
to intelligence, what human life is like without it.
Bring to mind the spineless person, who makes up
his mind about something but then changes his mind,
just because others disagree with him or do not approve of him for what he thinks, or who remains
inactive when the going gets rough. He thinks: "It's
a good idea to be healthy"—but he doesn't want to
eat carefully or exercise regularly! He thinks: "Friends
are good to have"—but he befriends nobody! "Education is a good thing," he agrees—but he cannot get
himself to sit down in a chair to study for at least an
hour at a time!

Do we criticize the person who "has no character"
because he gets nowhere? Yes. But we also realize
that he is missing so much of the zest and fun of life.
He is never creative. His trouble is not that he is only
a follower—although even as such not very dependable. It is that he will never know that wonderful
human experience of walking against the wind, and
making headway! He comes to be regarded as a
weakling and a social parasite, because he refuses to
be responsible for what is right and good.

To be sure, we often wish that life were not so
much a matter of decisions, decisions, decisions! But
again, to bring the issue right down to a basic choice,
suppose God had made you a successful machine, al-

ways running up to capacity—would you prefer life that way? Suppose God offered a choice between a life chock-full of pleasure, and the experience of making your own way; would you choose pleasure at the cost of free choice?

If you would, then I agree, God cannot for you be good in my sense of the word. For "good" means to you "good for my having pleasure"—no pain, no hardships, no insecurity. You seem to prefer security even at the expense of ever feeling, *"I really can make choices; I* can make my own way; *I* am creative within limits."

But consider a moment. Would you really say, for example: "I believe that the fish I caught, that I cooked well, does not taste better than the equally fresh one sent by my neighbor"? Would you really say: "The friends I made by my trust and co-operation are not better friends for that, and I am not the better for befriending them"?

If you would, I cannot argue further with you. I can only suspect that life must be for you as disappointing as a banquet to which you seemed to be invited as a guest with high expectations. The food turns out to be free but uncertain in quality and quantity. And your Host—your God—must be an uncertain joker. For if one thing seems sure in life, it is that there are few handouts, and even the "lucky people" who appear to receive them gratuitously are in the end handed the bill. No, I would argue, although I may be the one who is mistaken, that man is made *for* the struggle to create and *in* the struggle to create. The God upon whom man calls is "good" for him *in* and *for* the struggle, as inspirer and sustainer of creative man.

The rest of the argument depends upon this assumption, so we must bring possible differences into the open. We must, I suggest, face an ultimate choice unflinchingly. If we believe that security, at the cost of freedom and creativity, is the highest good, then, I would argue, we must say that God is not good. For the world we live in is clearly not made for security without creativity. Our Father worketh, and we work. And we sometimes work at cross purposes, with disastrous consequences and untold misery. Each of us acts often as if he were God omnipotent and omniscient—and we do it in the name of creativity and freedom!

Yet I would still argue that God is good because he puts character and personal responsibility ahead of passive acceptance and security. He is willing that he and we suffer when we abuse the powers that we have; he would rather risk seeing us hurt each other than not to know, at least within limits, what it means to be responsible. The world as a supermarket where the satisfactions of "gracious living" are purveyed unfailingly and securely, *or* the world as an artist's garret where independent souls strive toward the new vision God holds before them—which world would you really choose?

To summarize: I have been arguing that the life in which thinking is possible is in fact the life we would choose. We have recognized that to think is not easy, that success is not always forthcoming. This has led us to realize that thinking, and much else also in life, calls for character, the creative effort to stick to what we believe is best even in the face of insecurity and hardship. Life without thinking, without creativity, without the real risks and the zest that goes with these—such a life we would not exchange for a life of secure pleasures but lacking the zest of creativity and truth-seeking. But even these two basic sources of the things we prize highly in life do not exhaust the sources of human joy, achievement, and of possible sorrow!

3. Good—for Loving?

There is another kind of experience, another kind of creativity, that human beings must have if they are to grow. They need *to be loved* and *to love*. But "loving" and "being loved" can be destructive, and not creative, unless certain conditions are met. It is not just an accident that loving and being loved are, along with truth-finding and character, basic conditions of human growth.

Loving is not merely a matter of feeling highly emotional and favorable toward someone. If our love for others is not to hurt them, we must understand them, their capacities, their purposes, their wants and needs, their problems as well as our own. To be loving is to be creative in a special way. It is to gather up the powers we have for goodness and put them to work in helping others and ourselves to fulfill the potential we have together.

To be loved with imagination, on the other hand, seems to unleash power in us we never thought we had. Despite our sense of unworthiness we feel new incentive to grow. Loving and being loved gives us a zest for self-creation and for helping others to be creative; they encourage all that makes for additional good. They help us to live with evil in such a way that it will be overcome, or at least weakened as far as possible, in its power to hurt us.

We can see what is in mind here if we keep in mind our own development. Each of us was born helpless. Until we began to understand and do for ourselves, we needed kindness and informed care from our parents, brothers and sisters, doctors, and a host of others. Looking back over our lives, we know that when others cared for us *for ourselves,* when we could know that they were not simply using us, when they understood us and were willing to bear with our mistakes and, so often, with our meanness—it was at such times that we really respected ourselves and felt it worthwhile to try to be somebody. We can see ourselves as we would have been if someone else— mother, father, teacher, friend—had not believed in us even when our own mistakes and failures led us to lose faith in ourselves; we would have been poor, stunted creatures. Such grateful memories have their sting, too, when we ourselves use others selfishly, as mere instruments to our own satisfactions. We grew through the love we received. Our virtues, our successes, as we look back, came under such influences that we hardly know whether we achieved or whether those who loved us achieved through us. Thus, to grow ourselves in goodness and love is to allow not only our own personality but that of our benefactor, through us, to increase in effective power.

The Law of Human Growth

Do we need to add much more? These are some of the facts about ourselves we cannot neglect as we search for what gives the highest meaning to our lives. For these facts are facts about ourselves in this world. They are the laws of living with one another that we cannot escape any more than we can the facts of falling bodies. Love, like the sun, radiates everywhere and in unsuspected spots its power of growth.

Self-centeredness, however, exploits everything and everyone increasingly as tools for its own pleasure. Whenever we live with our own selves as the center, we may seem to grow in power, but we in fact become prisoners of our own success. For to use others is to despise them and at the same time to fear and distrust them. Increasingly, knowing that we have no right to expect them to help us, we have to fall back upon ourselves. We shrivel up as persons. On the other hand, to love, to trust others with understanding and respect, is to send our own personality abroad and to enjoy its freedom to work in, through, and with others. Thus we create a community of love.

But again, it takes hard, imaginative thinking and character to love so that the person loved will be strengthened. It takes a willingness to risk safety when one decides to forgive another who has purposely hurt him. Yet nothing less drastic than forgiving love will help the other to find himself, to master what makes him mean, and help him re-enter the community of respect-and-care. Nothing is more creative of good than love.

What It Means to Call God Good

If these things are so, do we not have another line of evidence to offer in answer to our question: Is God good? For have we not discovered another condition of human fulfillment in this kind of world? We have discovered the law that *there is no lasting growth of personality without love. Thinking and character are not enough in this kind of world. Human beings need to be loved and to love.*

All this we may represent in a triangle of values functioning in every high and lasting human good, a triangle of forces that must work together if they are not to destroy us, and yet without which our lives would be indescribably miserable.

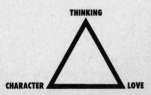

We have sought to describe the moral conditons underlying the most satisfactory human living. What may we infer from them about the nature of God? We have seen that when we call mother "good," we mean that she supports our highest values. She is good not merely because she has been the physical source of our lives but because she has supported us as we sought the values which made those lives worth living. Is God then not good in the same sense (as far as the analogy holds)?

If we live in a world where it is impossible for human beings to develop without thinking, character, and love, can we not conclude that so far as we know, "the grain of things" favors these as the foundation of our growth as persons. When we do not have the character to think or to love, we not only hurt ourselves but we hurt others; we run counter to the grain of our own natures and the "main sway" of things.

We could think otherwise if thoughtlessness, shiftlessness, and hatred were equally good for development of personality. But since thinking, character, and love help our natures to grow, make us appreciate each other and the world in which we live, why not say that these are God's main concern for us, the main conditions both for our living in a world we did not make and for developing our own original natures that we did not make. There is no good in us without thinking, loyalty to good, and being loved and loving. These are also the ingredients of our lives that give us deep satisfaction, and that we would not trade for an easy security.

What does it mean, then, to say that we believe in a good God? It is to say that we believe that the world is not an indifferent place in which any kind of living can flourish. Human beings have much freedom, but unless they are willing to discipline themselves courageously, in thought and in love, they are lost in this kind of world. To say that God is good is to say that the world and the persons he has created and sustains are such that they cannot be fulfilled without experiences of thinking, of creating, of loving. These three values are not only the keys to our natures and growth but the clues to what God is— Creator of the conditions that support love, thought, and character.

7

Is Everything God?

If the argument in the last six chapters has any merit, we can reasonably believe in a personal, good God. In other words, we can believe in a cosmic person, a mind that knows and plans the basic order of the world in which we live, and who cares about the part each of us plays or can play in relation to him and to each other. He made human nature so that we could make progress in knowing and appreciating his world, and so that we can share responsibility for the use of that world and for what happens to us as we live in it and with each other. We live in a world so grounded in wisdom and love that it encourages the development of persons through knowledge, character, and love (basically).

This faith may be mistaken, but it is not blind. Nor is it sentimental nor elaborately theoretical. It is a faith-for-living and it follows the model of our actual practice in other, not specifically religious, areas of life.

Isn't Conviction Based on Direct Experience of God Enough?

There are many who consider this whole approach unnatural. They will point out that much of the time we do not arrive at any of our important beliefs by so indirect an argument as the one that has been briefly sketched. We literally seem to jump to conclusions, and on the basis of some more or less direct experiences. I can almost hear them say: "God isn't an hypothesis to people who believe in him! No abstract argument like this is going to convince 'the average man' that there is a God!"

There may be some truth in this leap-to-belief theory of religious faith. It is also true that acts that seem direct and spontaneous have behind them a great deal of unthought-out experience, of listening, reading, and pondering. For example, the young man who "falls in love at first sight" is "absolutely convinced" that he has met "the real thing." He needs no argument to convince him that his girl is lovable, that they ought to get married as soon as possible, that all will be well. As a matter of fact, he may even feel a bit disloyal if he has to argue about, or seem to justify, his loving her. To be sure, if he is questioned about his love, he will try to dig up good evidence for his conviction that she is lovable and worth marrying. But what did the trick, he insists, was that electric moment in which she just magnetized every bit of him and gave him a new focus for living.

I would not for a moment deny that such a state of mind exists about "the beliefs men live by." These beliefs do not come at the end of a string of arguments; we debate about them, but the debate itself does not bring them into existence. There is certainly a lapse in time or logic between "falling in love on sight" and justifying that love, between "knowing in the core of my being that there is a God" and justifying that inner conviction. Still, can we deny that the person who has fallen in love has been prepared for this in good part at least by his past experience? Had he not been getting ready for love, if not for *this* girl?

I, for one, would be willing to go so far as to say that belief in God can come, be it after a long preparation or not, like love for a sweetheart; it can hit you "like a ton of bricks." At that moment the individual, however gradual or abrupt the process by which conviction comes, feels gripped by something beyond his power to direct or control; he is certain that he has "met God."

Is this, then, to make our case unnecessary? If God reveals himself in some electric moment, why argue about it?

I suggest we follow the parallel between falling in love and being convinced that there is a certain kind of God. People sometimes fall out of love as rapidly as they fall in; rapid or not, they just plain find themselves no longer loving the particular person who was "so lovable." There is no simple explanation of this, for every person's life experience is different.

But as two people have experiences together, they realize that they cannot meet each other's requirements for living. "He is not the man I thought he was. I see life differently now."

So also religious people, convinced that there is a God because "I experienced Him," have found themselves interpreting what he means to them differently. The God they fell in love with was not the God they thought he was. As their life experiences changed, they have not been able to agree with other sincere people about what God is and what he demands of them. They have done amazing things—good and bad—in the name of their beloved.

We come once more, then, to the need to think out what we believe, and to keep that thinking fresh—*no matter how we came to the belief.* We started this book on the challenge of growing minds that wanted to protect themselves from wishful thinking and from poor analogies when they did try to think of God. We have presented a line of approach to beliefs that gives a large role to reason. But there's no denying that *psychologically* the most convincing evidence for each individual comes in terms of some transforming experience in his life that makes his whole life, including whatever reasoning he has done, "come alive" *for him.* And when one has that kind of experience, "which has done so much for me," it is hard for him to accept the idea that what he believes at the time of "break-through" does not necessarily mean what he takes it to mean. He is like the lover who resists any suggestion that his present conviction and belief about his beloved may not be all there is to her.

Obviously, a great deal hangs on how "breakthrough" is interpreted, and I shall soon deal with this question. I have been interested only to show that one may prefer to follow the safer, if roundabout, way of reason and yet recognize that psychologically faith may seem a break-through. There is a moment of passion, in religion as in love, when to raise a question seems a betrayal. Yet religion, like love, in the end finds that more sober counsels may give passion staying power and new growth. As we shall now see, an underlying cleavage among believers in God is supported by both sides in good part by "break-through convictions" about the nature of God and his relation to man.

Is Everything One with God?

Personalistic Theism is the name we might give to the view of God that we have been suggesting. "Personalistic" emphasizes that God is conceived as a unified, thinking, willing, loving being. But "theist" means more than "believer in God" (as opposed to disbeliever—"atheist"). "Theist" emphasizes that the God believed in is not the same as the world and man, but is the creator of them. God's power and concern are constantly involved in his creation, but God is not identical with the world and man.

There are differences in detail when it comes to depicting God's relation to the world within the theistic camp. Some Theists, for example, urge that the world (not including man) is identical with God. God and non-human nature are one, but God and human minds are not identical.

Most Theists, however, hold that God "created" both the natural world (including physical things, plants and animals) and man. We need not stop to pursue these differences, for the important point here is that personalistic Theists hold that God is a cosmic mind or person having a life of his own, however "involved" he is in the world and man. No picture will do, but Diagram A, following, may help to emphasize that God is not identical with "all there is."

DIAGRAM A "Typical" THEISM
GOD: Cosmic Person created Physical World, World of Plants and Animals and Persons.

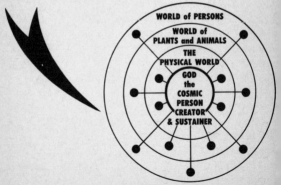

WORLD of PERSONS
WORLD of PLANTS and ANIMALS
THE PHYSICAL WORLD
GOD the COSMIC PERSON CREATOR & SUSTAINER

But within the Judeo-Christian religion (and especially in the dominant Hindu tradition, called *Advaita*) there is a strong denial of a creationist or theistic view, in favor of the contention that God, the world, and man *are* the Absolute Being. We must try to catch the spirit of this other basic way of thinking about God, or the Absolute, or the One. Other words, all emphasizing the identity of the world, man, and God are *pantheism* ("pan" meaning "all," hence "all is God") or *monism* (one all-inclusive being, not one who created others). The word "Absolute" is used to emphasize that God is the one, undivided, self-sufficient unity.

Again, there are differences of detail among pantheists. But they all agree in denying creation, because they think that all the different kinds of being, human and non-human, are expressions of the Ultimate One. While no analogy will do, we might approach their meaning by thinking of the way in which we could say that all of Shakespeare's plays are Shakespeare—different phases of his thought, emotion, and imagination; they could not, of course, exist apart from the unity of Shakespeare's life.

Another "model" might help. The notes in a musical composition are united by the musical theme, and each note has no meaning or existence apart from the theme (and the composer). We must not allow these analogies to lead us astray; the notes and the plays are "parted off" from the composer and the dramatist. But the Absolutist wishes to deny any "parting off," and to emphasize the inner vital unity of the One and all there is.

One other caution is important. God is not identical with things as *we* see them in our casual and practical way. Could we see the world from the Absolute's perspective, we would not recognize "our" world. For example, the city seen from an aeroplane bears some resemblance to the city as we see it on the ground—but what a difference! The details, with their individual life and color, are sacrificed to the pattern which holds them all together. All the streets are seen as an interconnected network; the houses and cars, which the observer knows as belonging to someone and important to someone, every one of them, are seen now more impersonally as parts of the total life and layout of the city.

No one way of expressing the relation of "the many" and "the One" will satisfy all Absolutists, but it seems both fair and emphatic to say that, for these thinkers, *all there is constitutes one whole of Reality, and that what we see as many seemingly separated and disconnected things and persons are One*. Because the One is all things, it cannot be identified with any aspect, part, or mode of the Being. Again, no picture will do, but to bring out the contrast with the theistic, Diagram B may help.

Now the interesting thing about this cleavage between the Theists and the Absolutists is that religious experience is used by each side as providing con-

vincing break-through evidence for the final truth of
its views. Both sides insist that, in the last analysis,
God "comes home" to the individual only as he feels
an inner assurance that God is that being "in whom
we live and breathe and have our being." Yet the

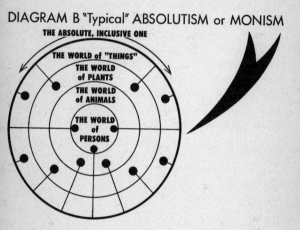

DIAGRAM B "Typical" ABSOLUTISM or MONISM

THE ABSOLUTE, INCLUSIVE ONE

THE WORLD of "THINGS"

THE WORLD of PLANTS

THE WORLD of ANIMALS

THE WORLD of PERSONS

difference between the two positions affects the interpretation of the "union" supposedly present in
religious experience, and this has important consequences for what each considers most important in
"the things that matter most." Let us take another
look through the pantheist's eyes, so that we may
better understand his emphasis.

What Does Religious Experience Mean? The Pantheist View

There is a level of religious experience, the mystical level, says the Absolutist, in which the individual feels at one with the Ultimate. In this religious experience he is not only "out of this world" but "outside himself." He loses all sense of self; his individuality is completely absorbed in the One. The word that can express the state of mind of one who has felt "the Life of all there is" as identical with his life, is "enlightenment," or perhaps even better, "awakening." The person who has had such an experience is a "new" man and sees all things in a new light.

No words can begin to express the ecstasy or richness of the actual experience felt by mystics of every religious tradition—such as the Buddhist, Jewish, Christian, Hindu, and Islamic. "Mysticism" carries for many people an impression of foggy mystery, but the fog is in the minds of everyone but the mystic. The mystics have no doubts about the reality; they have difficulty only in making clear to those who have not had this experience what they know with a clarity different from that "of this world." What the mystics of every tradition tell us is that once a worshiper can move beyond the world of his senses, he will behold a new world. It is something like what happens to a person who, having become shortsighted without being aware of it, now with proper eye-glasses sees "the world as it is."

The mystic's inner awakening is such that he never thereafter can give the world of our everyday sense experience the dominant place it usually plays in our lives. Indeed, he practices the art of keeping it from getting in the way of his getting back to "the real." Unlike the rest of us, he moves beyond the merry-go-round of "wanting this and that"; his supreme object of concentration will burn away or melt his desires. At the peak of his experience of "the One," he is caught up in a selfless ecstasy that defies description. No wonder he comes back to the ordinary life of his senses and his desires, and his logic, feeling that he has found something nothing on earth can ever replace. And, because it is the One that is "like nothing else," he sometimes says he has "found the great Nothing!" This may leave other people cold, but he who has known the experience yearns only to return to his deeper self, the real Self.

Every perspective in life is fraught with danger. What is the mystic's? Because his experience is so stirring and re-creating—because he now lives as a man who is "awake to the depths"—the things that matter so much to the rest of us who live on the sides or at the foot of the mountain, he tends to regard as so much clutter. So he becomes "otherworldly." He can become quite disdainful and contemptuous of "the world" as most of us see it. "Why stay here," he says, "why lose our hearts to 'this and that' when above us, but not beyond reach, towers the mountain peak of an unspeakable new life?"

The temptation of the mystics, then, is to be so disdainful of "the things of the world" that they are not willing to be "good citizens" in this world and accept the responsibilities of those who live with the bric-a-brac—no matter how glittering—of life. Nevertheless, the state they really aim at is not so much one of *un-attachment* to life, but one of *detachment,* of being "in the world but not of the world." This detachment, they say, can come only to those who, having been at the peak, know that what they come back to is not so important as it seems to those whose spirits have known only atmosphere, not stratosphere.

What Does Religious Experience Mean? The Theistic View

What does the Theist say to all this? He certainly does not deny that there are very profound and transforming religious experiences. He who has seen God will see every blade of grass, every animal, every human being, every "possession," in a new light; and he will be less likely to lose his heart to them. If the young man who has "met his love" sees all his old friends and all his other "attachments" in a new light, what may be expected to happen to the person who has "met his God" and has found his real "center"? Everything he has or knows is changed by his feeling of union with God. The new zest for living will not be diminished nor diverted by obstacles or sidetracks.

No, the Theist would not quarrel with "losing oneself in God" *as long as* this is not taken to mean that there is a real identity of the individual and God. Redirect one's desires, one's thought, one's whole center of spiritual gravity to God—yes, *lose yourself in the sense that you identify your good, your purpose, with God's.* But identify your own existence in every respect with God, consider yourself as part or a phase of God? No! Why?

I shall put in my own way and for myself the gist of the Theist denial of absolutism.

You *say,* one might reply to the Absolutist, that from the perspective of the Absolute the imperfections of life vanish. But you are really envisaging two situations hard to reconcile. On the one hand, you say: Take the imperfections of the world and of yourself as finite man seriously enough to overcome them by rising to a higher perspective! On the other hand, you say: Realize that somehow these imperfections don't really exist! In your view the One seems to be undreamt-of perfection and marvelous unity; but at the same time all the imperfections of nature, living things, and persons are part of that One—*in some sense.*

But whatever that sense is, if we are forced to say that imperfection, existing for us, does not exist in God, there are very serious consequences.

Thus, if all our failures and betrayals are perfected in the Whole, and with no additional cost to the Whole, do good or evil make a real difference? If, for example, we look squarely at both the suffering and the joy that are involved in human and animal existence, must we not say, on your absolutistic view, that all this suffering and the joy fit—with equal facility!—into the pattern of the One? If so, can it matter to such a One whether a million persons die of cholera or typhoid, or enjoy the zest of good health?

Furthermore, if everything we, as part of "this world," think is evil—like the destroying of innocent people—somehow is all right in the Absolute, what difference does it make what we think or do? No matter how we live, nor what we accomplish—in the One everything is all right regardless! Whether we pursue lives of hateful prejudice or of love, whether we destroy or protect each other's good, on your absolutistic view can either make a real difference? For our finite judgments, though said to be incomplete, must enter neatly and without strain into the life of the One.

To the contrary, as the personalistic Theist says, love, character, and wisdom we experience them are as real as anything else we experience. They are the foundations of whatever other good we human beings can realize. Likewise, hate, self-indulgence, and ignorance are ever sapping those foundations with just as much reality.

Let us, then, take another look at the experience of unity on which the religious Absolutist builds his case. We need not deny that the religious or mystical experience takes place. But any immediate feeling can give rise to more than one interpretation.

Granted that the sense of oneness is a religious state of mind that does have stirring and far-reaching effects. But that oneness can be interpreted as a "meeting of minds," as it were, and not a merging of minds. The unity is not at some deeper level of our being; *it is a unity, a harmony, of the purposes of different minds, finite and Infinite.*

Am I, a Theist, twisting the meaning of religious experience to fit the rest of my theory? The fact is that religious or mystical experience, as reported, is not dominantly an experience of unity in the Absolutist's sense. The words "face to face," "meeting," "encounter," or generally, "experience of Another"—a very different set of metaphors—are used to convey the "feel" for religious people of "the presence of God." God is a "Thou" over against human worshipers, but not identical in being with them.

To summarize the grounds for the Theist's rejection of Absolutism in the reverse order: The religious experience itself, as reported, is far from forcing an absolutistic One upon us. We should, in any case, hesitate to interpret it monistically. For we would be forced to think of God as perfect and imperfect at the same time. And what is equally bad, we would be deeply perplexed as to why normal judgments of good and evil do make a serious difference in our world if they make no difference in the One.

But even if these reasons for refusing to think of human persons as identical with God failed, the Theist would hold that the absolutistic view of God is inconsistent with the undeniable feeling of free choice each of us has so often. If we take our freedom of choice seriously—and also the sense of responsibility we feel because of it—the whole picture of the universe and our place in it changes, and we must then think of God as the Creator of creators. It is this theme that we must seek to understand in the last chapter of this book.

8

God as Creator of Creators

To Be Human Is to Be Free Within Limits

If human beings are really to be considered as drops of the infinite ocean of being, they can have only the freedom of choice and the sense of responsibility one would expect of such drops. That is, none at all. But to be a finite person is to be free, free to create good and evil, within limits. This is the fact on which the personalistic Theist builds his case against absolutism. It is also the fact that leads him to reject all views that reduce man to a tiny fraction of a Whole that alone has significance, or to a cog in a machine which is itself only a phase in the motion of a vast power system.

While arguments have been advanced on scientific, religious, and philosophical grounds for denying human beings their sense of freedom and responsibility for many of their actions, the Theist will not be dislodged. Man either has freedom or he is nothing. His freedom is within limits; yet it is a freedom to choose and make his choice stick. Otherwise, man is nothing. If he is only a puppet in a cosmic drama, unable to initiate changes in himself and in the world around him, he is of no consequence.

The fact of his freedom is dramatized in the biblical story of creation. Adam and Eve are free to obey or to disobey, to trust God or themselves. The Old Testament writer deliberately leaves other factors that affect man's choice in the shadow. The light plays on the free act itself. The divine command is made explicit, so that there can be no doubt of the meaning of man's own response. He can really will to obey or disobey.

Translating the biblical drama into philosophy, a conception of man begins to clear. Man is not a thing, obedient willy-nilly to the physical scheme of events; he is not an animal that, unable to think about what he is doing, is driven by his strongest desire to an inevitable act. In man we have a being not pushed here and there by the currents of power around him, not impelled by passion—though he feels the effects of both. No, he is not an image of things, nor of animals, but of God the Creator.

In the Absolutist view, on the other hand, man seems all the more religious if he depends, like a machine, upon the power house of which he is a wire. Such a view of man is often felt to be especially religious in its humility. Who is man that he should be able to resist the Absolute?

But one may doubt whether this view really honors God, whose glory no man disputes. Is it indeed a compliment to the Absolute to have man be a "center" of his power rather than a being endowed with the Ultimate's capacity to think and will for himself? If, furthermore, man is a puppet, men's worship of God is simply the reflection of his own light rather than the candle seeking to give its own light and warmth, however meager.

For the Theist, in other words, man is really to find God, love God, share God's purpose—with God's help, to be sure. But it takes two to find, to love, and to share; and worship of God is meaningless if man *is* God. If the figure that worships me from the mirror is merely my own image in one of its manifestations, there is no real worship, but self-worship. Real worship requires a distance and a difference! Better, then, says the Theist, to hold that God is never identical with man, or man with God. Better, then, to realize that it is God's purpose that man should fully harmonize his desires, thoughts, and actions to God's purpose and be one, in this sense, with God. But man can say no—even to God!

What Does Human Freedom Mean for God and Man?

It is one thing to affirm that man is free. It is another to be clear about what this freedom involves. There is much more here than meets the eye.* We must ask how the fact of freedom affects our thinking about man's dependence on God.

---

* See Peter A. Bertocci, *Free Will, Responsibility, and Grace* (New York: Abingdon Press, 1957).

Man and God are not one. But clearly man does not create his own being; that is, man does not create his own basic capacities to sense, remember, feel, think, will, and so on. For this basic nature, God is responsible. Moreover, God created man in a world whose basic constitution depends entirely upon God. The basic order of the world is controlled, not by man, but by God. God established the laws that govern the realm of matter and of life, including man's bodily power. God created man's mind and the principles it follows when the senses, memory, thought, and feeling are in operation. When man is free, he is not free to break the laws of sensing, remembering, and so on; he is free to *use them*, not to make them. But God does not govern or pre-ordain what choices man will make in using them. The choosing depends on man's own willing.

Thus man is free within limits. He is not free "to do anything" with either his body or his mind; by thinking he cannot add an inch to his stature or to his basic intelligence. But he can use his capacities and the ways of the world as he sees fit within these general limits.

The point to emphasize is that God will not bend man's will to do God's bidding. This means that both God and man take the consequences of man's choosing in an orderly world of physics, biology, and psychology. If man discovers the nuclear powers of nature as God made them, if he chooses to use them to destroy men, God will not interfere. God looked on as Abel died even though he disapproved of Cain's action in killing him. One brother perished according to God's law; the other brother was to feel the result of his action in his own nature, again according to God's law. Yet God's intention had been that they should live together as brothers and grateful children.

God, as both the story of Adam and Eve and that of Cain and Abel bring out, does not force his will upon men. God is responsible for man's freedom, for the opportunities open to their actions, for the laws men employ in the exercise of their freedom. But men are responsible for the way they use their freedom—and for the particular choices they make as to which of God's laws they will apply to their lives.

Again, God decides what laws operate when free action is taken; free action on man's part, however, does not make the laws according to which things change. Thus, if we pour concrete into a foundation it will harden and support a building of a certain size; that is, we decide which laws, governing what materials, will take effect on our foundations. It was God's original decision that this kind of substance should grow hard enough to sustain a certain weight; we are free to use it and take its consequences!

The Theist, then, affirms that man is free to choose, within the limits of his capacities. But the Theist is also careful to show how man's freedom is related to God's freedom and plan. Nor does he forget man's dependence on God, both for the freedom and for what it can accomplish. Man does not make the laws in accordance with which his capacities grow and develop and by which he affects other people and the world. God is responsible, as Creator, for the lawful and orderly world of nature and living things. God is responsible for the orderly process by which man's own body and mind develop. But, again within the limits of his capacities, man can choose what use to make of laws in his own nature and in the world outside of him. Man must, however, learn what these orderly processes are, and how they are connected with each other. He is free to make use of what he learns, but he is not free to change the nature of these laws or their consequences.

Thus we conclude: man is free in an orderly world, whose order he may use within limits for his purposes. *But he cannot escape from that order.* Without that order, in fact, his freedom—let alone his life—would be useless. For how would he know what to expect when he exerted freedom, if he could not depend upon certain things to happen as they have in the past—such as concrete hardening in a certain way?

To return to an earlier example: The astronaut is free to embark on his flight. But he embarks on it in the confidence, as we have said, that the sequence of happenings in space is predictable in the light of the sequence he knows on earth. Once in space he is free to choose only in the space environment; that is, his freedom is confined within the new environment to which he has exposed himself.

The same basic freedom-in-order is illustrated in the story of the prodigal son in Luke 15. The son is free to claim his inheritance—his father presumably agrees to give it to him under certain conditions. He is free to spend it in riotous living. But he is not free to save what he spends, and he is not free to escape the consequences of his life of riotous living. He is free to return home to his father, but what happens then depends on his father's character, wisdom, and love.

This last illustration from the realm of moral choice is of special point here. For it is easy to see that in the physical world our freedom must live with order and build new order if it is to be effective. But in the world of moral choice, we tend to act as if "anything goes"; we see freedom but not moral order. A closer look at the story of the prodigal son is instructive regarding *the freedom-in-order in moral development*. The son who is free to leave his father is not free to escape the consequences of his choice on his personality.

The existence of moral order in us and around us is not difficult to see. Does the man who chooses to be honest not generate the future? If a person allows himself to go on hating when more generous impulses are possible, must he not choose the consequences of hate in his own personality as well as in the person or persons hated? Kindness, honesty, courage, grati-

tude, meekness, humility, a sense of humor, independence, co-operativeness—all have their consequences both in our personalities and also in the social order they help to build.

Clearly, then, we choose—we create our own personalities on the basis of the capacities we inherited,
of our interaction with the world and persons, and of
our own past habits. But we can no more sow suspicion and reap gratitude and respect than we can sow
potatoes and reap corn. As we sow (in relative freedom), so shall we reap.

The Real World Persons Live in

Have we not come back by a different route to the
important points in our earlier argument for God?
We saw in Chapters 5 and 6 that the courage to live
by our best observations and thinking was the mini-
mum requirement for growth in knowledge. Yet
nobody is forced to be courageous; the scientist, the
astronaut, the repentant prodigal don't have to take
the particular course they take. But there would be
no point in being courageous unless one could depend on the results of choice. For freedom to succeed
is for freedom to depend on what is not free! Thus,
the scientist takes his freedom to experiment in hand
and is willing to risk his life, because he trusts, in some
uncertain areas, that "nature will not let me down."

Can we, then, reasonably draw two conclusions
from our evidence? First, if God is to make men
free, if God is to allow man to be a creator, he must

support him by creating a world that will remain orderly and dependable. We are free to eat bread only in a world where, as we eat, it does not turn to stone.

Belief in the freedom to choose one lawful sequence rather than another is basic to the theistic view of life. For God endows man with freedom—within a natural order and within a moral order. God leaves it up to man (within limits) to choose what particular order he will live in. If man chooses to live on the sides of volcanos, he must take the consequences of possible eruptions; if he chooses to live in a dog-eat-dog order, then he must accept the consequences.

Indeed, for the Theist, God's love for man consists in the very fact that He did create man free and with capacities for knowledge, character, forgiveness (and their opposites). The living God is loving, because he created co-creators. But man could create nothing without an orderly world in which to work and develop.

Second, we must rethink our picture of the universe. We do not live in two worlds, a physical world *and* a moral realm. Nor is the physical world one of dependable and strict interrelations, while the moral world is so loosely put together that "anything goes." *We live in a universe that expresses a moral order. We live in a world in which personal responsibility for action is as inescapable as the laws of nature. We live in a world in which the fulfillment and decay of persons is as subject to order as the stars in their courses.* The difference is that we are not forced by God to live in accordance with God's purposes for us as we are forced to live in accordance with the laws of gravitation. But we cannot escape the moral order any more than we can escape the physical order.

For example, we realize that if we are to grow good corn we must obey the laws for growing good corn. But we are tempted to think that we can corner the corn market as we please—no matter how self-indulgent we get or how many persons are undernourished. Yet, in God's purpose, the laws for growing corn and the ideals for human growth and community are not held apart. He will not force us to bring them together in our lives, for his purpose is that we should develop our own freedom and have the satisfaction of developing a society in which the strong help with the weak. But neither will he change his moral order to suit our whims or our selfish desires. In his world we are our brothers' keepers; if we do not fulfill that purpose, we slay each other—either all at once or in stages.

Again, if we accept the responsibility for discovering nuclear secrets but not the responsibility for turning these to peaceful purposes, we create a world in which constant fear and suspicion threaten, beyond the cold war, the explosion we all dread. Again, if we accept the responsibility for learning how people's minds function and are influenced but don't accept the responsibility for turning this knowledge into making better schools, homes, churches, and other social institutions, we may end up manipulating and "using" other people. And if we do, we may depend upon it: "The wages of sin is death" (Romans 6:23).

Thus we have a glimpse of the law of God *in nature and in man*. God, nature, man—this is the universe in which each of us lives. It is a world undergirded by thinking, self-discipline, and love. "In God We Trust" takes on a definite meaning. Without his thought and action in love, for the sake of our development as free persons, we could not grow in wisdom, character, and love.

The Meaning of Creation

God, on the theistic view, creates man and grants him limited freedom within order. We may now have a glimpse of "the way of life" this involves. But a very difficult question remains. How shall we understand the statement, "God creates"?

"Out of nothing" is the theistic answer. And what can this possibly mean? Let us see. The Theist does not deny that a mystery is involved here. But no contradiction is involved, as it would be if we said God is perfect and imperfect in the same way at the same time. Nor is the doctrine of creation silly, as it might seem on first glance. Why not?

To say that God created the world "out of nothing" does not mean, for example, that God took zero and made a million things out of zero. This doctrine, like many other religious doctrines which are dramatically expressed, must be understood as a *picture* of the essential situation and not as a literal description. It is intended to deny that God took something that he himself did not make—as a sculptor might take stone —and, as it were, carved the world out of it. Why the denial? What is so bad about God's taking something he himself did not make and creating the world and man out of it?

The puzzle is this. By definition, God (A) did not create "the stuff" (B) out of which the world is supposedly made. By definition also, B (the stuff) did not create A (God). If this is so, then presumably A and B had nothing in common. But if God and the stuff of the world had nothing in common, is it likely that God could make the kind of a world we have been talking about, or "matter" with whose nature he had nothing to do? If God had nothing to do with the nature of the "matter" out of which he presumably made the world, it is mysterious indeed that he could wield such an influence over it. Creation "out of nothing" is mysterious, but is it more mysterious than this ultimate *dualism* (two ultimate kinds of being)?

The Theist, we see, is in a sense caught between two positions, neither of which he can accept. If to avoid "out of nothing" he says with the Absolutist, "All is one and that One is God," he cannot explain the human freedom we have been talking about. Nor can he explain away the contradictions of saying that in some sense the perfect and the imperfect are one.

Such pantheism, we might say, explains the unity of the world so well that "the many" and their freedom become mysterious!

In order to avoid "out of nothing" and "the One," supposing the Theist tries the second position, dualism. He must then say: There are at least two ultimate beings (A and B). But A, our God, controls B in such a way that his order and purpose are done. But if, by definition, A and B had nothing in common, how comes it that God can have the upper hand, so to speak? We have not escaped mystery. And we now have two ultimates!

In this situation, the Theist can have no easy victory. He cannot blind himself to the fact that creation "out of nothing" is a mystery. But at least this mystery, once accepted, gives him a way of keeping unity, human freedom, and order among the many things that compose the world.

Thus, to say that God created "out of nothing" is to say frankly that we do not know *how* God created. God creates. *That is the ultimate—a certain kind of being, a Person, who creates.* This means that, as far as we can tell, in a world where once men did not exist, men did come into being.

And for reasons already given, we can hypothesize that God created man in the kind of world in which the order of things and the order of goodness are part of the controlling purpose.

For the basic act of creation, then, there is no model, no analogy, in the world. When God creates a person, a being is born that did not exist previously. But is there no order for God's creation? Perhaps what we have already seen about freedom and order may help here.

When men and women, following botanical laws, plant seeds, God gives the growth—that is, when men follow the proper conditions, acorns become oaks. Man does not make seeds grow; God creates oaks from acorns when certain conditions are met.

Similarly, when a man and a woman meet the biological conditions for a child's birth, God, in accordance with all the relevant biological laws and hereditary factors he has ordained, creates the infant. Again, he "giveth the growth" once the conditions are met, even if he himself might have preferred not to have that particular baby born at that time. But mother and father made use of God's order in accordance with their own limited freedom.

Further, if the biological laws and the laws of learning are followed, the infant will, under the conditions set up in the hereditary strain of the two parents, become what that infant can become physically and mentally. Later, as the child meets physical, mental, and moral principles—such as character, wisdom, love—he grows, under God's plan, into one kind of personality or another. At no point is he beyond God's concern, but he must decide which way his soul shall go.

To make the same point from a better angle: God does not select the mates; they "choose" each other and the time for child-bearing. Their moral choice, their knowledge, their self-discipline, their love, enter into the total process of bringing the child into the world. But God creates the child and maintains the world in which the child grows. In fact, God, the parents, and their society determine up to a point what the child's physical health, mental achievements, and moral purpose will be. As the child grows older, he also will enter into the process of development as a free agent. God, parents, society, and the growing person—they are the co-creators in God's world.

God, then, creates the original conditions of human existence. He creates creators who can choose within limits what their world, what their society, what their personalities shall be. He creates the conditions for fulfillment, but he does not force men to fulfill themselves. For he put the premium upon creativity and not blind uniformity. If men use their creativity to discipline themselves by wisdom and love, they share in God's creative joy. Such is the minimal theistic conception of the creation and growth of personalities.

Which God? Not God seen on the model of the potentate uninhibited in power, mowing down all opposition as would a jealous king. But God seen on the model of the loving Father, seeking in every way to help his children know what it means to know, to create, and to love. God seen on the model of a creator of freedom will accept the suffering when men deny him and hurt each other, but will never infringe upon the freedom. And as men draw near to him in repentance, he finds ways of helping them to recreate their lives in his world—this is the testimony of those who have committed their lives to him.

What Difference Does Belief in God Make?

To think about God, we now realize, is to think about basic issues that we all face as human beings. You and I may outlive our childhood beliefs, accepted from our parents and church at an uncritical age. But you and I do not outlive the problems that belief in God is trying to solve.

It is always reasonable to ask: Do our ventures in creating character, in living for a community governed by freedom and love, stand only for "the American way"? Or are they grounded in a reality common to all men? As we labor to throw back the veils of ignorance, are we simply adding some facts to other facts? Or do our efforts unravel an order that is the work of a Mind that co-operates with our best efforts?

We have answered that to believe in a personal God is to believe that in all of these ventures there is evidence of partnership. Our minds and their moral efforts, we believe, are not accidental and temporary efforts. Our individual lives are not interesting interludes between two oblivions. Each one of us is a creative agent in an orderly universe, planned by its Framer for creative co-responsibility.

Religion on this view is commitment to the conviction that growth of persons in knowledge, character, love, and other values is the very purpose of the universe. To believe in a personal God, therefore, is more than "to have an idea of God." It is to accept responsibility for every good that is in one's power. Religion gives, not security, but the capacity to undergo insecurity for the sake of knowing, loving, and creating.

When one commits his life to creative fellowship with his God and his fellow creators, a curious thing happens. He lives "beyond happiness," "beyond necessity." He feels it is more important to stand for growth in love, and to stand "on God's side" in the struggle for creativity, than to "be happy." Indeed, he becomes much too conscious of the sadness and the evil among men to think of life in terms of being either "happy" or "unhappy." The important thing for him is that he stop living as if he did not belong to the human race and to God. What happens to him is something that Nietzsche, opponent of all "safe" and "convenient" living, saw when he said: "He who has a *why* to live can bear with almost any *how*." The religious man is not "happy," for he has "peace that surpasseth understanding"—he feels *blessed*. Jesus gave stirring expression to the meaning of blessedness in the Sermon on the Mount.

This is not the place to indicate other far-reaching differences that belief in God makes, for this book is not a guide to practical religious living. But while the religious life must always be a vital fellowship between every man and his God, there will be dimensions of growth and responsibility if one joins with his fellow men in a church. He does not join the church for "social" reasons; he joins with his fellow men in seeking and finding the meaning of God in their life together in a community. His concern is not so much for agreement as it is that he and his fellow men participate in communion with God, and that they share in the responsibility for the coming of his kingdom in their hearts and minds.

Finally, each believer in a personal God will always live with his own honest doubts. He will also live, both in the church and in the community, with those who cannot honestly share his beliefs, either in part or as a whole. Both his doubts and his belief should make him humble and respectful. These are not idle words in our day, when even nations are placing their faith not in God but in ideals rooted, as they believe, only in man's life. No believer in God can betray that God by treating unbelievers as if they were not respected by God, and under God, indivisible with himself.

Discover all of these REFLECTION BOOKS

Each 50 cents unless otherwise marked